PSYCHOANALYSIS
OR
MIND AND MEANING

PSYCHOANALYSIS
OR
MIND AND MEANING

by

CHARLES BRENNER, M.D.

THE PSYCHOANALYTIC QUARTERLY, INC.
NEW YORK

Copyright © 2006 by The Psychoanalytic Quarterly, Inc.
Published by The Psychoanalytic Quarterly, Inc.
New York, New York
www.psaq.org
Editorial Assistant: Gina Atkinson

All rights reserved. No part of this publication may be reproduced or transmitted in any form or by any means, electronic or mechanical, including photocopying, recording, or by any information storage and retrieval, without prior permission of The Psychoanalytic Quarterly, Inc.

Library of Congress Cataloging-in-Publication Data:

Brenner, Charles, 1913–
   Psychoanalysis or mind and meaning / by Charles Brenner.
     p. ; cm.
   Includes bibliographical references.
   ISBN 0-9788040-0-7 (pbk.)
1. Psychoanalysis. 2. Psychoanalysis–Philosophy. 3. Conflict (Psychology) I. Title.
   [DNLM: 1. Psychoanalysis. 2. Conflict (Psychology) 3. Psychoanalytic Theory. WM 460 B838pa 2006]
   BF175.B7442 2006
   150.19'50–dc22
                        2006023602

Printed in the United States of America

TABLE OF CONTENTS

Preface	iii
Chapter 1	1
Chapter 2	11
Chapter 3	31
Chapter 4	47
Chapter 5	71
Epilogue	95
Appendix 1	97
Appendix 2	101
Appendix 3	109
Appendix 4	117
Appendix 5	133
References	139

PREFACE

In one sense, this book is a purely personal statement. In order to be clear in my own mind, I have tried to state as simply and directly as I could three things. The first consists of the conclusions I believe to be supported by the available, relevant data of observation about how the mind develops and functions. The second, based on the first, consists of the principles that I believe should guide the practitioner of psychoanalysis as a form of psychotherapy. The third consists of the data of observation on which I base the first two.

Although undertaken for my own sake, my publishing this book indicates that I hope it will interest others as well and that some, at least, will find it worth their time and effort to learn my thoughts on these matters. But this is not all I hope for. My more important reason for publication is to encourage those of my analytic colleagues whose conclusions differ from my own to present their ideas about the theory and practice of analysis both fully and directly and, what I believe to be of utmost importance, to present the data of observation that, in their opinions, support the generalizations they believe to be correct. Theories without reference to the data that support them leave much unsaid that must be said if one is to evaluate the theories themselves with any degree of confidence in one's ability to do so.

If psychoanalysis is part of natural science, as I maintain it is, there is no room for mutually contradictory theories about how the mind develops and functions. Each theory that is put forward should be the best conclusion one can reach on the basis of the observable, relevant data. There is room for disagreement about whether a particular theory is indeed the most plausible; about what data are relevant and compelling; about whether it is supported or contradicted by other than analytic evidence, i.e., by evidence not derived from the psychoanalytic situation; and so on. But there is no room for what is called pluralism in psychoanalytic theory. Any theoretical conclusion is either acceptable as valid in the light of present knowledge or it isn't. One doesn't have to look for a unitary theory. One's task is simply to winnow the wheat from the chaff, to save the one and discard the other.

That is what I believe is the most important message of this book. What I hope is that those colleagues, of whom I have no doubt there are many, who disagree with the conclusions I have drawn from what I believe are the available, relevant data about how the mind develops and functions, will do what I have tried to do here: to state their conclusions/theories as I have tried to do mine and to follow the example I have tried to set of being explicit about which data they believe support their theories and why. Those who read can decide for themselves which theories they believe to be valid and why and which to discard, either provisionally or definitively, as invalid.

I believe that one must go back to the writings of Freud himself to come up with a plausible explanation of the fact that analysts, with rare if any exceptions, haven't specified and discussed the observational data that, in their judgment, validate their theories of mental functioning and development. The fact is that Freud was disinclined to do so and those who came later seem to have followed his example. The one major exception, as far as Freud is concerned, is his discussion of the repetition compulsion (Freud 1920), which I have summarized at length in chapter 2. There he was at pains to give a detailed account of what he took to be the evidence that he believed supports the theory that mental functioning, though following the pleasure/unpleasure principle to a large extent, is even more importantly guided by a tendency to repeat events of the past. Elsewhere he was not.

One can only speculate about why Freud followed this practice. But whatever the reasons, he unfortunately set a bad example by not being explicit about the data on which he based his theories. It is high time that we depart from it.

I remember attending a seminar while still a candidate at the New York Psychoanalytic Institute that had as its focus for discussion the very question I've just raised. The instructors were three eminent members of the faculty: Heinz Hartmann, Ernst Kris, and Lawrence Kubie. Kubie maintained that psychoanalytic theories have no factual evidence to support them, other than analysts' intuitive understanding of what their patients say and do. Hartmann and Kris thought otherwise. In support of their view, I volunteered to summarize the evidence that Freud presented about a repetition compulsion, the result of which pleased them, though I'm sure it never convinced Kubie.

It will be apparent in what follows that the theories about mental development and functioning that I believe to be valid are the ones that seem to me to best explain the relevant data about mental development and functioning that are known to us at present. As far as they are concerned, there is nothing new in this book. I have written it all before in one article and book or another over the course of many years (e.g., Brenner 1982, 2000, 2005). But here I have collected it all in one place, so to speak. It was a task to do so, nonetheless—a task that has constituted my principal professional activity for more than two years. In fact, I can say that every sentence, if not every word, has been carefully considered, written, and rewritten.

What is new is that, throughout this book, I have tried to be specific about the data on which I base my conclusions. I believe that those conclusions should be accepted by everyone in the field because they are the ones that, in my opinion, best fit the available, relevant data. If someone can come up with theories that better fit the data or with relevant data that are new or that I've overlooked or neglected and that demand emendation of the theories I've presented, I'm ready to make whatever changes in theory are necessary. I have no personal interest in any of them. What I do believe, however, is that it is not acceptable to take the position that "You have your theories and I have mine, and each of us is entitled to prefer his or her own to those of anyone else." What's desirable, what's necessary, if you will, is that all those interested in the subject get together and reach consensus about what are the available, relevant data, about what theories fit the data best, and why. When that is done, the pluralism that plagues psychoanalysis at present will no longer be a problem. It will be clear what is agreed upon, where disagreements lie, and why. At the present time, consensus is out of the question. But the first step toward achieving some degree of consensus is to be clear about the differences. If the differences about theory and about technique are clearly presented, and if the supporting evidence for each is made evident, analysts will be in a position to form a judgment about the validity of the many divergent conclusions about theory and technique that abound in current psychoanalytic thought and writings. A consummation devoutly to be wished.

A word about the somewhat unusual format I have chosen. To have included the appendices—or their essence—in the main text would, I believe, have interfered with my exposition and made it more difficult to follow. I recommend that the reader ignore the appendices until after having read each chapter and go back to them only after having first read through the chapter without interruption.

CHAPTER 1

"When *I* use a word, it means just what I choose it to mean!" As with Humpty Dumpty in Wonderland, so with psychoanalysts today. All use the same word, but those who use it don't always mean the same thing. It means what each chooses it to mean. Nearly all practice a form of psychotherapy they call psychoanalysis. Most refer to their preferred theories about how the human mind develops and functions as psychoanalytic theory. Many belong to the International Psychoanalytical Association or are connected with some branch of it. They read, or glance at the same professional publications and attend meetings and conferences labeled psychoanalytic. But what goes under the heading of psychoanalysis, both in theory and in practice, is fascinatingly diverse.

In what follows, I shall not attempt to review in any systematic way the literature on the diverse meanings of the word *psychoanalysis*. I shall attempt only to explain as fully and as clearly as I can what I choose to mean when I use it and my reasons for having made the choices I've made.

By analogy with the diversity in the spheres of politics and international relations, the differences that characterize psychoanalysis are frequently referred to as *pluralism*. To many analysts, pluralism is welcomed as evidence of open-mindedness and a lack of intellectual arrogance. To some, it is the target of thunderous anathemas. What some approve, others condemn.

Condemnation and approval are interesting phenomena. When pronounced by psychoanalysts, they often include some reference to Freud. One hears statements to the effect that so-and-so is or isn't a true Freudian, where "a true Freudian" is a term of approval and "not a true Freudian" is the opposite. In the opinion of other colleagues, just the reverse is the case. For them, "Freudian" is a term of disapproval and "non-Freudian" or "post-Freudian" one of approbation. I suggest that both usages serve only to cloud discussion. It is not only unnecessary to approve or condemn one theory or another in Freud's name, it is disadvantageous as well. Whether one greatly admires Freud or not is beside the point in any discussion of psychoanalytic theories and practices. Freud proposed certain theories concerning the nature and development of mental functioning, as well as ideas concerning the most useful ways of studying mental functioning. Some of his theories and ideas he himself rejected in the course of time, usually replacing them with new ones that seemed to him more useful and better in accord with the data available to him.[1] He never asserted that his conclusions were exempt from review or, where indicated, from revision. Psychoanalytic theories and practices, whether they were proposed by Freud or by some other analyst, should be discussed and evaluated on their merits and on their merits alone. To use or misuse Freud's name either as a blessing or its opposite is beside the point. The question is how to winnow the wheat from the chaff. What is valid should be retained as part of analytic theory. What is not valid should be put aside either definitively or provisionally. Such are the rules of science, which psychoanalysis, as a branch of natural science, should follow.

But matters are not so simple. Not all analysts agree that psychoanalysis is in fact a branch of natural science and as such should follow the rules of science. Could they be right? Could it be that psychoanalysis is, perhaps, a humanistic or a philosophical enterprise and not a scientific one at all?

The theory and practice of psychoanalysis were dominated by Freud during his lifetime and for many years thereafter to an unusual degree. He devised the method, which he called the method of free association, and he made most of the great discoveries in the field. It was his opinion that psychoanalysis is a branch of natural science and that basic to psychoanalysis is the scientific view of the world. For all or nearly all analysts of the time, that settled

---

[1] For examples, see appendix 1.

the matter. Psychoanalysis was considered to be what Freud said it was, a scientific enterprise. At present, if one can judge from the literature on the subject, there are more than a few analysts who maintain that psychoanalysis is a form of textual analysis, a kind of exegesis of what a patient communicates during each analytic hour. Others maintain that psychoanalysis is only a protoscience at present, that the data available through the use of its method of investigation are too unreliable to serve as a basis for any valid conclusions about how the mind works. Still others believe that ideas, because they are immaterial, are not part of the physical world, so the study of ideas, which is the task psychoanalysts set for themselves, cannot be part of natural science, since natural science deals with material, physical phenomena. Then there are analysts who maintain that "truth" is but a relative concept. Post-modern science, according to some analysts, postulates that there can be many truths, some mutually contradictory.

Such differences are important. They affect the way one understands and practices analysis. An analyst who considers analysis not to be a branch of science may depend primarily on intuition and may not be much interested in appraising evidence for or against an interpretation. One who considers "truth" to be unattainable may not bother to try to establish the facts of a patient's mental development. Any appealing narrative will do. If one thinks that ideas aren't part of the physical world, one may tend to derogate the importance of bodily factors in a patient's mental life. One may be inclined to talk and think almost exclusively of relationships and of interactions.

Because theories are so varied at the present time and because theory influences practice in such important ways, I shall begin my discussion by a consideration of the question of whether psychoanalysis is or is not a branch of natural science. It seems to me to be necessary to do so before proceeding to any further discussion of what I have to say about the theory and practice of psychoanalysis.

What is "science," anyway? What is meant by the term? How can one define or describe it?

Science is conventionally defined according to subject matter. One branch of science is physics; another is chemistry; others are biology, geology, astronomy, and so on. Such definitions are perfectly adequate for purposes of classroom and departmental division, but only a brief reflection is necessary to realize how inadequate they are when it comes to trying to define what science is. Science is much more than a matter of different disciplines or topics. The subject matter of science is the entire universe, including our own bodies and minds. The concept of *science* is only definable as a way of looking at the world and, more importantly, of trying to understand it. For practical purposes, *science* is less a noun than an adjective. It is a way of looking at as much of the world as is available to us. It is an attitude toward the entire universe, an attitude that is characterized by certain beliefs that distinguish it from other ways of looking at the world.

There are, after all, many different ways of looking at the world. The scientific way is only one way to understand it. Each of many religions has its own way of doing so, and so do mysticism, animism, a belief in magic, or a belief in leprechauns or fairies (Farrell 1955). Adherents of each believe that its explanation of the world is the best. And like each of them, science has its own beliefs, its own credo. Those who are guided by it believe that one can best understand the phenomena of the universe by using the best available methods of observing those phenomena, by following rules of logic, and by not tolerating mutually contradictory explanations or supernatural, magical, or ad hoc ones. It is a credo that has proved to be a very fruitful one since the time it was first proposed, some four hundred years ago, by Francis Bacon in his *Novum Organum* (1620). So fruitful, indeed, that by now it commands the full belief of many, and what one might call partial or conditional belief from nearly everyone. Modern technology, based on scientific knowledge, commands universal respect.

A corollary of this definition of science has to do with the meaning of the word *truth*. An important feature of the scientific credo is that there is no such thing as an immutable truth. It is part of the scientific credo that any conclusion drawn from observation of whatever part of the universe is under scrutiny is to be called true or valid if, and only if, it is the best possible explanatory formulation of the available, relevant data of observation.[2] If one is scientific in one's approach to understanding the world, this definition of truth applies equally to profound and esoteric theories and to an understanding of why a patient was late to an analytic appointment. Each is "true" or "valid" if it is the best possible conjecture with which to understand the available, relevant observations.

It should go without saying that there will be many instances in which one's judgment is that the available, relevant observations are too few or too uncertain to give one confidence that any conjecture or theory about them is valid, just as there will be others where it seems impossible to prefer one conjecture to another and where judgment should be deferred. It is equally obvious that a conjecture that seems valid to one observer (analyst) may be judged invalid by another. The point I wish to make is that, according to the scientific credo, facts reign supreme. If newly discovered facts demonstrate the inadequacy of what, until then, had been a theory accepted as valid, the theory must be altered or discarded to take account of the newly discovered facts. Facts, not theories, are the court of last resort in science. The story is told that a theologian once responded, when confronted with the logical absurdity of some of his beliefs, "I believe *because* it is absurd" ("Credo *quia* absurdum"). That's all very well if one's credo is that of a religion that accepts the validity of miracles. It's not possible if one subscribes to the credo of science.

There are analysts who object to granting validity to psychoanalytic conjectures (usually theories of general import, rather than conjectures about the meaning of individual clinical observations) on the grounds that any conjecture is too much influenced by an analyst's own conflicts or blind spots to be granted validity. In fact, however, *every* scientific theory or conjecture is determinatively influenced by the theoretician's (or clinician's) conflicts. This is a

---

[2] See appendix 2.

problem in every branch of science and in every therapeutic endeavor, not just in psychoanalysis. The decision about the validity of any explanatory formulation must be a matter of judgment. In some cases, there is consensus and in others, not, but for every such formulation, whether psychoanalytic or other, a judgment must be made and each person's judgment is necessarily influenced by that person's conflicts.

There is a widespread idea that the words *hypothesis, theory,* and *law* have different meanings in the language of science. They don't. Conjecture, hypothesis, theory, law—they all mean the same. They all mean the best conclusion that can be reached in trying to understand something about the world on the basis of the available, relevant facts. The definition of each of the words is identical. It is only the connotation of each that is different. When a conclusion of this sort has been repeatedly tested by many observers over a long period of time, it's apt to be called a law, while the other words usually indicate a somewhat less certain conviction about the validity of the conclusion, whatever it happens to be. But no conclusion is immune from contradiction or revision, however well enshrined it has become. Whether it be called conjecture, hypothesis, theory, or law, if new facts are discovered that contradict it, it must be altered. A new conclusion must be framed to replace it.

Another objection to the validity of psychoanalytic theories or conjectures is that many of them are inferential. For example, the question is asked by some, "How can you be sure that there really are unconscious thoughts and feelings? You can't ever observe them directly. They're only an inference." Like the previous objection, this is a problem in every branch of science, not just psychoanalysis. It is perfectly true that a belief in the presence and importance of unconscious thoughts and feelings in mental life is an inference. That doesn't make it invalid. The test of the validity of any psychoanalytic proposition is whether it is the best conjecture that can be made on the basis of the available, relevant data, just as is the case in any other branch of science. For example, physicists have inferred the concept of *force* as an explanatory theory from many and various observations. The concept is purely inferential. A force can no more be observed directly than can an unconscious thought, but both are valid inferences from the available, relevant data. What one can *observe* as a physicist are the effects of an inferred something that is described as a force and that one concludes, on the basis of one's observations, makes billiard balls and other objects behave as they do at times. Just so, as a psychoanalyst one observes people behave and at the same time report their thoughts in a way that leads to the conclusion that they are motivated at times to act because of thoughts and feelings of which they have no conscious knowledge. How better to explain the well-known fact of posthypnotic suggestion, for example? Both the concept of force and the concept of unconscious thoughts and feelings are "true," i.e., they are valid propositions (= theories) by scientific criteria. They are supported by many available, relevant data and contradicted by none.

Bear in mind also that every scientific theory is conceived by and subscribed to by human beings. None is revealed from on high, according to the scientific credo. Each is the product of a human imagination. Every theory, whether psychoanalytic or other, is shaped by a person's wishes, conflicts, and fantasies, unconscious as well as conscious. As I shall discuss at some length later on, this is the way people's minds work, whether at work or at play. It's inevitable that influences from each person's past—childhood wishes and compromise formations—play a role in each person's scientific endeavors. They play the same determinative role in everything everyone does. The question is not whether a given conclusion is free from personal bias. No conclusion ever is or ever can be. What the scientific credo requires is not freedom from personal bias when it comes to theory formation. What it does require is that the theory fit the facts, that it is the best conclusion that can be drawn, the facts (= data of observation) being what they are.

The experience of the past four hundred years indicates that when this condition is met, the resultant theory deserves to be called *valid*. It is that experience that is the basis of the conclusion that adherence to the scientific credo is the best (= most reliable and useful) way of trying to understand the world of which we are part.

Two other objections that have been made to the assertion that psychoanalysis is a branch of science should be mentioned here. The first is that psychoanalysts don't use the experimental method. The second is that the theories and conjectures of psychoanalysis are qualitative, not quantitative. Critics who raise these objections assert that, to qualify as scientific, any method of investigation must utilize the experimental method and must make use of mathematics. According to this line of reasoning, since psychoanalysis fails both tests, it cannot be considered scientific.

No one can deny the importance of both mathematics and the use of the experimental method in the development of science as we know it today. To recognize their importance, however, is not to say that either has always been essential to every scientific discovery in every branch of science. One has only to think of how important observation, as opposed to experimentation, has been in astronomy, as, for example, in Galileo's observations on the sequential changes in the positions of the moons of Jupiter. Telescopic observations are not experiments, but they can be very important as data on which to base valid, scientific theories.

As for mathematics, it is a language, not a science. It is a language that is invaluable when applicable, one that is as useful in the logical analysis of many problems as verbal language is in its sphere. It is not, however, essential either to scientific observations or to scientific conjectures. As an example, I refer again to Galileo's conjecture, based on nonmathematical observations and expressed in nonmathematical language, that the moons of Jupiter revolve about that planet. Mathematics is a way of thinking —a language—that is often invaluable, but not always so. The tools one uses in any branch of science are determined by the nature of the problems one faces. There are no tools that fit all. Nor can one predict which methods and tools will be the right ones. Who could have predicted, before Virchow and Pasteur, that the use of the compound microscope would be such a valuable tool in the study of the diseases that afflict mankind or, before Fraunhofer, that the spectroscope would be so useful in the study of the stars?

A further word on the subject of the relation between psychoanalysis and science is this. The brain is the organ of the mind. Until one and a half or two centuries ago, it was arguable to think of *mind* and *body* as somehow separate. Not so today. No one familiar with the findings during these relatively recent years in the fields of neurology, psychiatry, neurophysiology, comparative psychology, neuropathology, psychopharmacology, developmental psychology, and embryology can doubt that mental phenomena —what is called the *mind*—are an aspect of cerebral functioning. The age-old belief that human beings are a duality, one part the immortal spirit and the other the mortal body, is no longer a tenable hypothesis. All the relevant evidence that is currently available supports the conclusion that mind is an aspect of cerebral functioning, as surely as respiration is an aspect of pulmonary functioning or circulation of cardiac functioning. The study of the mind, both in health and illness, is, therefore, part of biology and, as such, part of natural science.

To repeat, an analyst should, in my opinion, accept as valid the conclusion that psychoanalysis is a branch of natural science, and that the development and functioning of the mind are best understood if one subscribes to what I call the scientific credo. That means using the best (= most suitable) methods of observation, following rules of logic, and not accepting explanations (= theories) that are ad hoc, or that depend on a belief in magic and supernatural powers, or that are mutually contradictory.

In conclusion, the word *science* is more adjectival than nominal. It refers to a view of the world and to an attitude on the part of those who subscribe to it that may be called *the scientific credo*. Applied to the theory and technique of psychoanalysis, it means that analysts should have a scientific attitude toward the facts they observe and try to understand. Psychoanalytic technique and psychoanalytic theorizing should be governed by the general rules that govern all scientific endeavor. There is no room in them for ad hoc explanations, for ones that are illogical or mutually contradictory, or for ones that depend on magical or supernatural assumptions.

CHAPTER 2

So what are my ideas about the branch of natural science called psychoanalysis?

Meaning

To begin with, there are two general aspects of mental functioning that must be kept in mind. The first is a very simple one. It has to do with that property of thought that is called its meaning. Implicit in what has been said till now, as well as in what will follow, is the thesis that the meaning of a thought or idea is of utmost importance. The realization that every neurotic symptom and every parapraxis has a meaning was, in fact, one of the earliest discoveries about the mind that is owed to psychoanalysis. I emphasize this because it is an aspect of what Freud discovered so early that has not received the explicit attention it deserves. This is perhaps due in part to the fact that, in his own writings on the subject, Freud seems to have been inclined to put more emphasis on the intensity of the wishes involved in conflicts—their cathexis, as he called it—than on their meaning, and in part to the fact that he was steadfast in his belief, despite evidence to the contrary, that there are patients with what he called *actual neuroses* whose attacks of anxiety have no meaning, but are due instead to unhygienic sexual practices (see Brenner 1953).

Whatever the reasons, the result is regrettable. It is true that, for practical reasons, the *meaning* of a psychic symptom may at times be neglected as unimportant. For example, when a patient with a high fever is delirious, what is important is to treat the cause of the fever, not to try to understand the meaning of the delirious thoughts. If, however, in a psychotherapeutic situation, a patient is disturbed without such an obvious nonpsychological cause, it is incumbent on the therapist, in my opinion, to try to understand the meaning of whatever the patient's symptom(s) may be. Every thought and action has a meaning.

It is likewise meaning that determines the effect of external stimuli on the mind. A soft sound in one's ear that conveys no special meaning is of little consequence. A sound of the same intensity that conveys a meaning can have a profound effect on mental functioning. Its meaning may be such as to cause one to weep, to laugh, to faint, to run, to strike—in a word, to do anything that body and mind are capable of doing. It is the meaning that is of the essence. It matters not what words or language are used to express the meaning; it is what those words and language *mean* to the listener—what their *meaning* is—that counts.

Causation/Psychic Determinism

The second point I wish to make explicit is that thoughts and actions are linked together in sequence by their meaning. To say that each element in a sequence of thoughts and actions *can* be linked together in a meaningful, cause-and-effect way is nothing new. A bit of introspection is all that is necessary to demonstrate that they can be. However one chooses to define them, cause and effect *can* play the same sort of role in mental life as they do in the physical world around us. What psychoanalysis, and psychoanalysis alone, has demonstrated is that the connection between the meaning of one thought or action and the next is not just *sometimes* one of cause and effect. There is *always* a cause and effect connection. Thoughts are never random, although they may, of course, be influenced by perceptions either from the external world or from one's own body, especially by sensations of pleasure or the reverse.

The fact that thoughts are causally connected, the fact that cause and effect apply to mental phenomena, is what Freud (1901) referred to as psychic determinism. Whenever someone is willing and able to communicate his or her thoughts and feelings without reserve, i.e., whenever thoughts can be studied by the psychoanalytic method, it becomes apparent that what seem to be instances of random and unconnected thoughts are the result of motives of which the subject is unaware. The meaningful cause is always there, whether or not it is immediately apparent to the speaker, the listener, or both.[1]

The Pleasure Principle

Both personal experience and simple observation support the conclusion that the mind works in such a fashion as to gain as much pleasure as it can and, at the same time, to avoid as much unpleasure as possible. As Freud conceived and phrased it, the mind is regulated by the pleasure/unpleasure principle (for short, the *pleasure principle*). But simple observation also indicates that, at least for adults, to experience unpleasure can be a state of mind that is highly prized and sometimes even actively sought, as, for example, in asceticism. If the pleasure principle really characterizes all of mental life, how is one to explain those situations in which a person accepts or even seems to seek unpleasure and/or to avoid pleasure?

Freud made at least two attempts to answer this question. His first answer was based on what he learned from his clinical work. In neurotic patients, the *conscious* desire for unpleasure and/or the apparent avoidance of pleasure serve to mask or deny *unconscious* pleasurable gratification and avoidance of unpleasure in the form of punishment or retaliation, either real or fantasied. In such cases, the pleasure principle is seen to still govern mental functioning, once one takes account of unconscious and otherwise hidden factors.

But in the course of time and, no doubt, as his clinical experience grew, Freud became dissatisfied with the idea that the pleasure principle, i.e., an effort to achieve pleasure and to avoid unpleasure, always governs the way the mind works. In 1920, he proposed a new theory in a book he called *Beyond the Pleasure Principle*. According to his new theory, it is a compulsion to repeat

[1] See appendix 2.

that basically governs all of mental functioning. The repetition compulsion encompasses the pleasure principle, according to Freud's second theory, and goes beyond it.

I believe the second theory is not valid. In order to support the correctness of my conclusion, I shall begin by outlining the data Freud set forward in support of his idea of a repetition compulsion.

Repetition Compulsion

Freud began with a description of the dreams of many patients with traumatic neurosis. In their dreams, these patients, over and over again, relived with anguish the events that caused the onset of their symptoms. These patients, said Freud, seemed to be under a compulsion to repeat their traumatic experience, whatever it might have been, despite its highly unpleasurable nature.

He next called attention to the fact that young children repeat over and over, in their play, experiences that were highly unpleasurable, just as patients with traumatic neurosis may do in their dreams. As an example, he described the behavior of a year-and-a-half-old boy (in fact, his own grandson) who repeatedly enacted in play the unpleasurable experience of his mother's leaving him.

A similar tendency to repeat what is unpleasurable, said Freud, is apparent in the behavior of patients in psychoanalytic treatment. In their transference, they reenact in relation to their analysts the highly unpleasurable, even traumatic, fantasies and experiences of early childhood that still plague them in their adult lives. He referred also to persons whose whole lives seem guided by an inexorable tendency to repeat some tragic, highly unpleasurable situation. Although Freud in 1920 did not consider these individuals as neurotic, in later psychoanalytic literature they were classified as "fate neuroses." They repeat situations that give rise to unpleasure in their lifelong behavior, much as patients with traumatic neuroses do in their dreams and as children may do in their play.

In presenting all this evidence that he thought supported the theory of a repetition compulsion, Freud also pointed out that none of it was conclusive. With respect to the dreams of patients with traumatic neurosis, he noted in a second edition of *Beyond the Pleasure Principle* (Freud 1920) the possibility that they may be manifestations of masochistic wishes. In a later work, he wrote that:

> In view of all we know about the structure of the comparatively simple neuroses of everyday life, it would seem highly improbable that a neurosis could come into being merely because of the objective presence of danger, without any participation of the deeper layers of the mental apparatus. [Freud 1926, p. 129]

With respect to the repetitive play of his one-and-a-half-year-old grandson Freud suggested that the boy's throwing away his toy, which represented his mother's departure, might be an act of revenge, with the meaning, "Go away! I don't want you!"—in which case the repetition would carry with it a yield of pleasure of a very direct sort. In fact, Freud (1920) wrote in his original exposition that there is no need to "assume the existence of a special imitative instinct [= repetition compulsion] in order to provide a motive for [this sort of] play" (p. 17). However, despite his reservations, Freud concluded this section of his work as follows:

> On more mature reflection we shall be forced to admit that . . . the whole ground is not covered by the operation of the familiar motive forces [i.e., an attempt to achieve pleasure and to avoid unpleasure]. Enough is left unexplained to justify the hypothesis of a compulsion to repeat —something more primitive, more elementary, more instinctual than the pleasure principle which it over-rides. [1920, p. 23]

My own opinion is just the reverse. Freud (1926) himself pointed to the fact that no case of traumatic neurosis of the sort he described had ever been analyzed (p. 129), and such cases, he wrote in 1920, are the ones that offer the most plausible support to the theory of a repetition compulsion. Children's play, patients' behavior in the course of analytic treatment, and the fate neuroses offer even weaker support. To accept a theory with such far-reaching implications on such a dubious basis seems to me unjustified. Simply on the basis of Freud's presentation thus far, it seems to me that the theory of a repetition compulsion is invalid.

Freud's attempt in 1920 to demonstrate the inadequacy of the pleasure principle and the validity of the theory of a repetition compulsion did not end with the discussion I have just outlined, however. The major portion of *Beyond the Pleasure Principle* is in fact devoted to a development of the idea (= theory) that, in order to explain human mental functioning satisfactorily, one must postulate two basic drives, a life drive and a death drive, both of which demonstrate the fundamental role of the repetition compulsion. In particular, the death drive, Freud argued, offers strong evidence in favor of the view that repetition is more important in mental life than are the attempts to gain pleasure and avoid unpleasure. His evidence for this is of particular interest because it is not psychological in nature. It has nothing to do with observations made by using the psychoanalytic method of investigation. His argument ran as follows: All living organisms eventually die. They are formed in the first place from inorganic, i.e., not living, chemicals, and when they die, as they must do, they become once more inorganic material. It is as though the return to an inorganic state is a kind of repetition, a repetition compulsion that is a tendency of all protoplasm, including, of course, mankind.

It is difficult for me to understand what relevance this argument, if valid, has to human mental functioning. It seems to assume that *metabolic* processes in protoplasm must necessarily be reflected or repeated in *mental* processes, an assumption that is dubious on its face. But beyond that, the very idea that there is a course that all living organisms take from lifelessness to life and back to lifelessness is invalid in light of our present knowledge. There is no such difference between *organic* (= living) and *inorganic* (= lifeless or dead) chemicals, as those names imply and as was once thought to be the case. It was once thought that some chemicals are found only in living plants and animals or in their excretions. In 1830, a chemical, urea, which was thought to be organic in this sense, was synthesized. This proved to be just the beginning. Since then thousands of other "organic" chemicals have been synthesized as well and the view that there is a fundamental distinction between organic chemicals and inorganic ones is a view that has steadily lost ground and that has been, by now, completely discredited. Today, as for many years past, the term *organic chemical* means only a compound that contains one or more carbon atoms. Organic chemistry is not the chemistry of living organisms. It is the chemistry of compounds of carbon, no more and no less. And there is no sharp line that distinguishes those chemicals of which carbon is a constituent, and which we customarily call *living*, from the ones we customarily call *lifeless* or *dead*. Some chemical entities have properties to which the term *life* or *alive* is customarily given, while others do not, but there is no sharp division between the two. To use a familiar term (though not really an explanatory one), they form a continuum. All are compounds of carbon.

The fact is that the terms *alive* and *dead* are ones whose meanings are wholly psychological. Physicochemically, they merge into one another. As psychoanalysts and, for that matter, in everyday thought we distinguish sharply between what is alive and what is dead. The two concepts have clearly distinct meanings from one another in common parlance, but the distinction is based on our own, nonscientific ideas about life and death. It is not one that is based on a knowledge of differences in molecular structure, i.e., on other than psychological evidence. Current data about the chemical structure of clusters of molecules that are called living and those that are called dead support the conclusion that there is no sharp dividing line between the two. There is, for example, no definable point at which a living organism dies. There is a gradual progression, as far as chemical structure and properties are concerned, from the one state to the other. The terms *living* and *dead* have obvious meanings psychologically, but there is no such clear difference between the two for a chemist. One cannot support a theory of a death drive (or a life drive) and a repetition compulsion on other than psychological evidence and that is what Freud tried to do: to support a theory that there is a compulsion to repeat that overrides the pleasure principle and that is based on nonpsychological evidence. Which is why I consider Freud's theory of a repetition compulsion and of life and death drives to be invalid. All the currently available, relevant evidence speaks in favor of the conclusion (= theory) that the mind always works to gain as much pleasure as it can, and, at the same time, to avoid unpleasure insofar as it is possible to do so. This is the essence of what Abend (1994) has aptly labeled *modern conflict theory*.[2]

Mental Conflict and Compromise Formation

Granted that this is the case, there are inevitably times in everyone's life when one wishes for something that is intensely pleasurable either in fact or in fantasy, but which is, alas, also associated with intense unpleasure. What results in such a situation is what is meant by the concept of *psychic or mental conflict*. In a situation of conflict, the mind reacts in accordance with the pleasure principle. It achieves as much gratification of the pleasurable wish as is possible without too much unpleasure. To use familiar psychoanalytic terminology, what results is a *compromise formation*.

My observations have convinced me, as has been the case for many other psychoanalysts beginning with Freud, that the conflicts that are the most intense and the compromise formations that are the most fateful for mental functioning throughout the course of every individual's life are those that center on the pleasure-seeking sexual and aggressive wishes of early childhood (Freud 1905, 1926). This is a conclusion of major importance to the theory of mental functioning. As such it demands discussion.

The sexual and aggressive wishes referred to make their first clearly identifiable appearance in mental life at about the age of three years. They constitute what Freud (1905) called *infantile sex-*

---

[2] See appendix 5.

uality. His attention was drawn to them by the observations he made on his adult patients who were in analysis with him, but recollections of childhood in adult life are only one of the classes of data that support the conclusions he drew. Anyone who takes the time to observe young children's behavior and to listen to what they have to say can confirm Freud's conclusions. The pleasure-seeking wishes in question are essentially the same as those that characterize the sexual lives of adults. Young children yearn for the attention of other persons, particularly their parents, and for the stimulating pleasure of physical contact with them. They are jealous of any rival. They intensely resent any evidence of infidelity, lack of interest, or neglect on the part of the person(s) they yearn for. They desire revenge, whether against a successful rival, the faithless loved one, or both. Being ignorant, they are curious about what adult sexual partners do to each other and with each other and wish to do the same themselves. Being relatively small, weak, ignorant, and unintelligent, they feel inferior and humiliated and, in turn, miserable, desperate, and enraged at feeling so. They intensely desire to be grown-up men and women who are as clever, wise, and sexually successful as the adults around them seem to be. With respect to its psychological side, in fact, a child's sexual life is in full flower by the time he or she is four or five years old, long before reaching puberty and the beginning of physical sexual maturity.

But young children, ages three to six years, are not independent creatures. They are dependent on their caregivers—usually parents—not only physically, but emotionally as well. Parental love, physical contact, approval, admiration, protection, and all that go with them are of utmost importance as sources of pleasure before, during, and after that time of life. Contrariwise, anything that—in a child's mind—forfeits or threatens to forfeit parental love and approval, anything that a child believes will turn one or both parents against it or has already done so, becomes a source of intense unpleasure. High on the list of such sources of intense unpleasure are the child's own sexual and aggressive wishes, since many of these are directed toward its parents, against its parents, or both. What develops, in other words, is psychic conflict. Every child, by the very nature of things, finds itself wishing for things that are intensely pleasurable in fact or fantasy and that are also associated with intense unpleasure. Its sexual and aggressive wishes become associated with intensely unpleasurable ideas of disapproval, rejection, abandonment, retribution, and punishment by its parents. That association, that concatenation of pleasure and unpleasure that is the essence of psychic conflict, is an inevitable feature of the mental life of every child. The outcome is what is called *compromise formation:* a thought and/or action that is, in part, the pleasurable gratification of a sexual and/or aggressive wish and, in part, a way of avoiding the associated unpleasure by means of defense and self-punishment.

Chronology

But why just at this time of life? Why not earlier, as many analysts believe is the case, or, for that matter, why not much later, as other analysts maintain?

In order to answer these questions there are certain features of the development of the brain that must be taken into account.

The brain, particularly the forebrain, is the organ of the mind. In humans, the brain is far from fully developed, both anatomically and functionally, at birth. Both in interaction with the environment and as a matter of genetically determined heredity, it continues to grow and change in many aspects of its functioning, of which the mind is one, until well into adolescence.

Evidences of this are legion. As an example, the normal electroencephalogram (= EEG) of a neonate is very different from that of an older child or adult. It could easily be mistaken for that of a comatose adult. As another example, in many children, the eyes at birth do not move in a coordinated fashion. Each moves independently of the other for the first several days or weeks of life. In these children, the neurons that will later coordinate the movements of the two eyes are anatomically and functionally not yet fully developed at birth. As still another example, the cells of the precentral gyrus, the so-called motor cortex of the brain, don't begin to control the movements of the limbs till a number of months after birth, regardless of how sturdy and well developed a baby may be. This is clinically evident in the fact that the plantar reflex (= Babinski's reflex) of a neonate is the same as the plantar reflex of an older child or adult whose motor cortex has been destroyed by illness or injury to the brain. It's not until about the age of one year that the brain normally develops to a stage at which it is capable of initiating and controlling coordinated movements of the limbs in the way that is normal in later life.

What is equally striking and of greater relevance to the present discussion are the progressive changes in language capacity that result from the growth and development of the forebrain in the months and years after birth. During the first several months of infancy, the human brain is an organ that is functionally incapable of acquiring language. It's not a matter of the baby's not having had as yet sufficient time, experience, and practice to acquire language. Practice and experience are necessary for the acquisition of language when the brain is functionally capable of doing so. Before that time it is impossible. When that time comes varies from individual to individual, the median age being about a year. It takes that long for the brain to develop anatomically and functionally to the point at which it has become an organ capable of acquiring language. Even then, it takes months and years of further growth and change for the capacity for the acquisition of language to develop fully. No child can read or write, for example, until the brain has grown anatomically and functionally for several years after birth.

All of this has major consequences for the way the mind functions after the age of three years or so. There is every reason to believe, and none to doubt, that the *desire* to achieve pleasure and to avoid unpleasure are features of mental life well before the age of three, but *thoughts with meanings* of the sort that lead to conflict are not possible in the mind of a person whose brain has not yet developed to a stage at which language and language-dependent thoughts are possible.

It is only after the age of three years or so that a child can begin to have such thoughts as, "If I get rid of the baby, mommy and daddy will do something terrible to me," or "Why can't I get rid of daddy and be in bed with mommy? Maybe it's because my penis is too small," or "Why can't I have/make a baby too?" or "They hate me because I want to do such bad things," and so on. Before that time, before a child's brain has matured sufficiently, thoughts of that sort are impossible. Beginning at about that age, such thoughts, and the conflicts to which they give rise, are inevitable.[3] There can be little doubt that, long before they are three, children desire to be physically close, feel happy at times and unhappy at other times, loving, angry and so on. Mental life surely doesn't begin at age three. But wishes and conflicts of the sort described do begin then. They cannot begin earlier, nor can they be postponed till later. They make their appearance when the brain has matured anatomically and functionally to a degree that makes it possible for the child to have the meaningful language to frame such complicated wishes, joys, fears, and miseries. It is then that compromise formation develops in accordance with the pleasure principle and proceeds to take its position in mental life at center stage.

Thus, from a very early time in every person's life, beginning at about three years of age, there is a constant effort directed both toward seeking satisfaction of sexual and aggressive wishes of childhood origin, and toward minimizing the very unpleasant consequences that are associated with them. Along with the pleasure-seeking wishes come associated unpleasurable thoughts—the fears and miseries of early childhood. The action of the mind in at-

---

[3] The term *oedipal* is customarily used to distinguish the wishes and conflicts that distinguish ages three to six from those of earlier and later times of life. The word has the advantage of both familiarity and dramatic impact, but it has serious disadvantages as well. Infantile sexuality includes far more than a young boy's wish to kill father, marry mother, and have children by her, which is what Oedipus did, according to legend. The use of the term *oedipal* to designate the sexual wishes and conflicts that characterize that age has not infrequently led to the misunderstanding that they are limited to the wish to do what Oedipus is supposed to have done.

tempting to achieve the pleasure of satisfying its sexual and aggressive wishes, and at the same time to avoid the unpleasure that is necessarily associated with them, is what is meant by conflict and compromise formation. Each child's conflicts and compromise formations are unique, but no child can avoid having them. As Freud (1905) pointed out long ago, they are a consequence of the fact that every young child is so dependent, both physically and emotionally, on the parents, and that sexual physical maturity, as well as general physical maturity, are so long delayed. Thus, the contents of mental conflict are sexual and aggressive wishes and their associated fears and miseries. The age at which these conflicts make their appearance and first flourish is, roughly, three to six years. They are an inescapable feature of human mental development.

What more should be said about them? I have already described the wishes that are involved. What gives rise to the unpleasure that, in the course of the fateful years, three to six, becomes associated with them? It's clear that they arouse emotions of pleasurable excitement and gratification. What are the unpleasurable emotions (affects) to which, during those years, they also give rise?

Theory of Affects

My attempt to answer this question requires that I say something about affects in general. How can affects be defined and understood?

The theory of affects that I shall present is based on psychoanalytic data. It asserts that affects are complex mental phenomena that can best be understood in developmental terms. Their antecedents are sensations of pleasure and unpleasure, the most important of which are those associated with gratification of pleasure-seeking wishes and with lack of gratification of such wishes. Those pleasurable and unpleasurable sensations are the matrix from which the entire gamut of the affects of later life develop (see Brenner 1974a, 1974b, 1974c, 1975).

At an early stage of psychic development, memories and other ideas become associated with the sensations of pleasure and unpleasure connected with pleasure-seeking wishes. The resulting complex of sensation and ideas is an affect. Any affect includes (a) sensations of pleasure and unpleasure or a mixture of the two, plus (b) thoughts, memories, wishes, fears—in a word, ideas. *Ideas and sensations together constitute an affect* as a psychological phenomenon. Whatever the affect, either the pleasure-unpleasure sensations, the ideas, or both, may be wholly or partly unconscious or otherwise warded off.

Pleasure and unpleasure are sensations. We assume, probably correctly, that like other sensations they are a genetically determined part of mentation from the beginning of mental life, whenever that time may come in the chronology of the development of the brain. They are urgently important at that time and they remain so, as far as is known, without essential change throughout the rest of life.

The developmental history of the *ideas* that are part of every affect is obviously very different from the developmental history of the sensations of pleasure and unpleasure. The *ideational content* of every affect at any particular stage of mental development is determined by the functional capability of the brain at the time, as well as by the influence of previous experience—i.e., by memories of past experience and by fantasies past and present. As far as present knowledge goes, the development of affects from infancy to adult life means the development of the ideas that are a part of affects. It is the ideational content that changes and that accounts for the differences between primitive affects and those that are more mature—between those often called *global* and those called *discrete* or *differentiated*.

Classification of Affects

With these developmental considerations in mind, one can attempt to distinguish each affect from the others and to classify them. The most natural beginning is to separate affects characterized by sensations of pleasure from those characterized by sensations of unpleasure. However, it must be remembered that, in any particular case, such sensations may be repressed and/or otherwise defended against. An affect that is consciously perceived as pleasurable may, when examined with the help of the psychoanalytic method, prove to include hidden or disguised unpleasure and vice versa. For this reason, a classification such as the one suggested should include a third category, namely, affects characterized by a mixture of pleasure and unpleasure.

In each of these categories, affects can be classified on the basis of their ideational content. Granted that the ideational content of an affect is always unique in the sense of being specific for each individual, and that for each individual the ideational content of an affect will vary from one stage of development to the next, nonetheless, there are general similarities as well as differences. For example, any pleasurable affect whose ideational content is that of gratification of a (pleasure-seeking) wish can be called *happiness*. If the sensation of pleasure is intense, one might call the affect *ecstasy* or *bliss*. If the ideas have to do with having defeated a rival or rivals, one may call the affect *triumph*. Depending on the intensity of the pleasure and the nature of the ideas, one might define varieties of triumph as *omnipotence, self-satisfaction, mild superiority, smugness,* and so on.

Thus, speaking generally, one can define pleasurable affects and distinguish them from one another on the basis of the intensity of their pleasurable sensation and the content and origin of their ideas. Unpleasurable affects may be similarly defined and distinguished from one another on the basis of the intensity of their unpleasurable sensation and the content and origin of their ideas. Among these, the affect that has been most often and most extensively discussed among psychoanalysts, beginning with Freud, is anxiety. How is anxiety to be conceptualized and defined?

In accordance with present knowledge of affects in general, anxiety is unpleasure plus ideas that have to do with danger. Anxiety is unpleasure plus a set of ideas, one of which is that something unpleasurable is about to happen. As was described in the case of happiness, different labels can be used to indicate variations both in the intensity of the unpleasure and the nature of the conscious and unconscious ideas making up the affect. If the danger is perceived as acute or imminent, one can speak of *fear*. If the unpleasure is intense, of *panic*. If the unpleasure is mild and the danger perceived as slight, uncertain, or distant, the affect can be labeled *uneasiness* or *worry*, but if an affect is to be labeled as some form of anxiety, it should include in its ideational content an anticipation or expectation that something bad is in the offing.

In this connection, one must bear in mind in one's clinical work the fact, already mentioned, that anxiety, like any other affect, can be unconscious as well as conscious. Every analyst is familiar with the fact that, for example, the unpleasure of anxiety may be unconscious, even though the ideational content is largely conscious (= isolation of affect). Equally familiar are situations in which the unpleasure is conscious in large measure, but the ideational content is unconscious or otherwise warded off. Whenever a patient is conscious of no unpleasure in connection with thoughts of danger, an analyst looks for the reasons why. Whenever a patient is unaware of what it is that he or she fears, one's analytic efforts should be directed toward the questions, "What is this patient unconsciously afraid of?" and "What are the origins of this patient's fears?" But whatever the balance may be between what is conscious and what is unconscious, anxiety, like every other affect, is never without ideational content. "Pure" anxiety is a fiction. When the analytic method can be applied, the ideational content of anxiety can be discovered, as can the ideational content of any other affect.

Pleasure and unpleasure are often mixed. For example, a patient who was an actor by profession complained of stage fright. Before any performance, he was aware both of pleasurable, anticipatory excitement and of an unpleasurable affect whose ideational content was that the performance he was about to give would be a dismal failure. A pleasurable affect and an unpleasurable one were conscious at the same time. In other cases of mixed affect, however, either one or both may be unconscious or otherwise defended against, and in fact clinical situations are usually quite complicated in this respect, as one might anticipate. Pleasure and unpleasure, gratification and calamity, are closely intertwined.

In such complex situations, which make up so many of the affects in adults with which analysts are faced in their work, it matters little whether one speaks of a mixture of affects or speaks of affects that are in themselves mixed, as I suggested earlier. The difference is more one of terminology than of substance. In addition, one must realize that affects are never precisely the same in any two persons. No two persons can ever wish, fear, regret, or remember precisely the same things. Different persons' affects have common elements that can serve as a basis for classification, but no more than this can be meant when affects are named and classified.

The Role of Depressive Affect in Conflict and Compromise Formation [4]

Anxiety—the idea that something unpleasurable will happen in the near or distant future—is not the only unpleasurable affect that is part of mental conflict. Depressive affect—misery—is another. As surely as every child experiences anxiety in connection with its sexual and aggressive wishes, just as surely does every child experience depressive affect in connection with them. As Freud (1926) discovered long ago, the expectation of calamity can cause conflict and compromise formation in childhood, but so can the conviction that calamity has already happened, that it is a fact of life. In some conflicts, the defensive activity is not motivated as much by a desire to avoid some calamity as it is by a desire to reverse a calamity, to undo it, to prove that it never really happened. When, in analysis, one attempts to understand a patient's conflicts and to convey that understanding to a patient, this fact must be taken into account. It doesn't do much good to try to demonstrate to a patient that they're afraid something terrible, whatever it may be, is about to happen when in fact what is responsible for the pathological compromise formation (= symptom) is a conviction that it's already happened—that they've already been despised or abandoned or castrated.

[4] See appendix 3.

Anxiety, Depressive Affect, and the Calamities of Childhood

The calamities of childhood, whether feared or experienced as facts of life, are infinite in number, if one takes into account the fact that their specific nature is unique for each child. When one looks for similarities on which to base some generalization concerning them, the one suggested by Freud (1926) seems to me to be the one that is best. He classified the "something bad" that either threatens or is a fact of life under three broad headings: abandonment, loss of love, and physical injury or defect, in particular injury or defect with respect to the genitals. The last is what is meant by the psychoanalytic term *castration* (Freud 1926).

It should be borne in mind also that part of the ideational content of each of these three calamities is the idea that the calamity in question is a parental punishment or retribution. In other words, thoughts of parental approval and disapproval are an important aspect of the ideational content of each of the calamities of childhood. Children don't think just, "I'll be [or I am] all alone," they think, "Mommy and daddy will leave [or have left] me all alone." And the same for each of the other calamities. It should go without saying that all three calamities are often, perhaps always, intertwined. Every child suffers to some extent from all three.

When a sensation of unpleasure is accompanied by the idea that a calamity is neither a matter of the future nor of the past, but is actually happening at the moment, it is difficult to know whether the affect is better classified as anxiety or as depressive affect. Sometimes the one seems preferable, sometimes the other. For example, a child may feel, "Mother doesn't love me any more." This would be an affect characterized by unpleasure and the idea of a calamity in the present. For one child, however, the calamity in the present may have the ideational content, "She doesn't love me. She stopped long ago when [her] baby came," or, "She stopped yesterday when I wished she was dead." For another child the present calamity may have the ideational content, "She hates me. She doesn't love me any more. She will never love me again."

The first instance would be an example of depressive affect, in the opinion of most observers. The second would be classified by most as an example of anxiety. I think, however, that all would agree that it makes little difference which label one applies to either—which is to say that anxiety and depressive affect can, at times, be indistinguishable varieties of unpleasure plus ideas about the occurrence of one or more of the calamities of childhood in the present.

When that is the case, when the distinction is merely an academic one, there is nothing to be gained by trying to decide whether the affect in question is better classified as anxiety or as depressive affect. In the great majority of cases, however, the distinction between the two is clear, and in those cases, it is of great practical importance to reach a decision as to which affect is involved. It makes a significant difference to one's understanding of a patient's conflicts if the patient's unpleasure has to do with impending calamity, i.e., with danger, or if it has to do with a calamity that has already happened, i.e., with misery (= depressive affect), or, as is often the case, if it has to do with both at the same time. When one classifies an unpleasurable affect as anxiety, one means that ideas of calamity are in the future, that the present situation is one of danger. When one classifies an unpleasurable affect as depressive affect, one means that the calamity has happened in the past, that the present situation is one of misery and suffering as a result.

Defense

The method(s) used to mitigate the unpleasure that is part of the ideational content of any of the calamities of childhood are what are called *defenses*.[5] It is essential in clinical work to realize that the methods of defense include whatever the mind is capable of (Brenner 1973, 1976, 1982). The idea that there are special *defense mechanisms* (A. Freud 1936) is both erroneous and poten-

[5] See appendix 4.

tially misleading. Any of the familiar list of "defense mechanisms" (repression, reaction formation, projection, identification, and so on) can be, and at times is, used as a means of achieving pleasurable gratification. And any "mental mechanism" can be, and at times is, used for defensive purposes. When a mental mechanism is used defensively, one may label it a *defense mechanism,* but one must always keep in mind that there are no mental mechanisms that are especially, much less exclusively, used for defensive purposes. Even a pleasure-seeking wish and/or behavior can be used defensively—as, for example, a heterosexual wish to defend against a homosexual one, or a tender, loving wish to defend against a murderous one, as is the case in reaction formation. And even repression, traditionally thought of as the defense mechanism par excellence, can be used in the service of gratifying a pleasure-seeking wish, as well as in the service of defense.

CHAPTER 3

As was noted in chapter 2, the pleasure-seeking sexual and aggressive wishes that give rise to conflict and compromise formation are already in full flower by the time a child reaches the ages of three to six. Anyone who takes the time to observe young children's behavior and to listen to what they have to say with an unprejudiced mind can confirm that this is so. But how about the statement that these wishes and their real and/or fantasied consequences motivate every thought and action throughout life? What are the data that support the conclusion that those conflicts and compromise formations don't simply disappear as children grow older, but persist and continue to play such an important role in mental functioning forever, in everyone's life?

The question is not whether compromise formations resulting from conflict over the sexual and aggressive wishes of early childhood *can* persist and play an important role in later life. The development and application of the psychoanalytic method have made it abundantly clear that in some cases they can and do persist into later life in the form of neurotic symptoms. The question is whether they play the same or a similar role in all later mental functioning. Is such conflict ubiquitous? Is it as much a feature of those aspects of mental functioning that are conventionally called *normal* as it is of those that are conventionally referred to as *pathological* or *neurotic*?

The evidence that they are ubiquitous comes both from analytic and nonanalytic data of observation. Analytic evidence very early convinced Freud (1901, 1917) that the inadvertent slips and errors of daily life are due to the same sorts of conflict as those responsible for his patients' neurotic symptoms, despite the fact that such slips occur in everyone's mental functioning, not just in the minds of those labeled *neurotic*. In fact, he called such slips "the psychopathology of everyday life," for the very reason that they bore the same relationship to conflict as did his patients' symptoms. Both are compromise formations.

For other aspects of normal, waking mental life, however, the view persisted for many years that conflicts of the sort referred to are not involved. The evidence for the contrary view that, in fact, conflict is ubiquitous, that it characterizes every thought and action, that it is as important a determinant of what is conventionally called *normal* mental functioning as it is of what is called *pathological* mental functioning, can be divided into two groups, analytic and nonanalytic, according to whether or not it is evidence collected by the use of the analytic method in an analytic situation. Analytic evidence has a unique advantage: analysis is the best available method for studying the determinants of any particular thought or action. Analytic evidence is the most reliable available evidence. Unfortunately, it has a disadvantage as well. Psychoanalysis is a method of therapy. The analytic method is mostly used to study thoughts and actions of the sort conventionally classified as neurotic, i.e., thoughts and actions called *abnormal* or *pathological*. Examples of analysis of thoughts and actions that everyone, or nearly everyone, would agree should be called *normal* are not too plentiful. Nonanalytic evidence has the advantage that examples abound. It has the disadvantage, however, that the evidence furnished by those examples is less reliable.

I shall start with a few brief clinical vignettes to illustrate my thesis. The first patient was a woman in her mid-twenties who came to analysis because of rather severe neurotic difficulties. Conspicuous in her lifestyle was her generous devotion to charitable causes. Analytic data demonstrated that this character trait was as closely connected with psychic conflict as were the symptoms of which she complained, yet it was clearly not to be classified as pathological. Her charitable generosity gave her conscious pleasure. It was not self-injurious, nor did it bring her into conflict of any serious degree with either her family and close friends or with society in general.

The patient had been separated from her mother repeatedly and for long periods of time, beginning very early in childhood. As far back as she could remember, moreover, her relation with her mother was frustrating and unhappy for the patient, and the circumstances of the many separations suggest strongly that, from the very earliest months of the patient's life, the moody, self-centered, undependable woman who had borne her was a most unsatisfying parent.

The patient's intensely ambivalent ties to her mother and the conflicts they engendered were of principal importance in every aspect of the patient's neurotic symptomatology. In addition, they were the principal determinants of her devotion to charitable causes. From a very early age, the patient was the protector of her younger siblings, babes as forlorn as the patient herself and as exposed to their mother's unpredictable moods and rejecting behavior. Though she was only slightly older than the others, she championed them, argued their causes, tried to shield them from punishment, and solaced them in distress, as though she were herself their mother, rather than their sister. She acted toward them throughout her childhood and adolescence as a good mother should behave to her children. Later, in adult life, the patient experienced and lived out the same urge to help the poor, mistreated ones of the world of which she had now become a part. She had an urgent need to help those whom she called the little people of society and took great satisfaction in doing so, giving generously of her time, her effort, and her money. Those she succored were unconsciously equated with herself and her siblings as children. Those she hated were unconsciously equated with her mother.

Thus this patient's devotion to certain charitable causes was identical with a neurotic symptom in being a compromise formation resulting from conflict over sexual and aggressive wishes that had their origins in early childhood. Among the wishes were longing for mother's love and attention, murderous rage at her mother, and murderous jealousy of her siblings. Each of these wishes was modified by defense, so that, instead of being aware of a yearning for her mother's love, she acted the loving mother to the objects of her charity. Instead of rage at her mother, she was angry at the establishment that oppresses "little people." Instead of being jealous of the little people, she took pleasure in being generous to them as she had been to her own siblings from as far back as she could remember. In addition, in her charitable work, she was actively in charge rather than helpless, frightened, and miserable. She was good, not bad. She shared instead of being greedy and selfish.

Brief and condensed as it is, I believe that this vignette illustrates that this patient's normal character trait of charitable generosity was just as much a compromise formation resulting from conflict over the sexual and aggressive wishes of her childhood as were her neurotic symptoms.

Another illustrative example has to do with choice of vocation. This patient was a young physician in his thirties. He had been separated from his mother for several weeks when he was in his fourth year because she was hospitalized for a major surgical procedure. This event had many consequences for the patient's development and later life. Among them was the patient's decision to become a physician—in fact, a surgeon, a doctor "who cuts 'em up," as he thereafter told anyone who asked him what he was going to be when he grew up.

Here again, it is clear that a normal aspect of a patient's mental life—choice of vocation—was a compromise formation. Wishes, anxiety and depressive affects, defense, and self-punitive tendencies are all involved as determinants. In addition, this case is of special interest because we have clear evidence indicating that the compromise formation in question began between the ages of three and six. The patient was three when his mother was hospitalized and he remembered wanting to be a doctor as early as the age of five.

My third illustrative example is a 30-year-old man who was characteristically cheerful, pleasant, sensible, diligent, and cooperative. His good spirits involved no conscious effort. They came to him as naturally as breathing, it seemed. He was, in fact, the product of a well-bred, highly moral, upper-middle-class family and of the best schools, and he behaved as such a person is supposed to do.

The aspect of his personality that I have just described was certainly a normal character trait. It was socially acceptable, it often served him well in life, and it caused him neither pain nor distress. He had his moments of discouragement from time to time, as everyone does when failure or danger threatens, but with him, these emotions never lasted very long. He would quickly adopt the sensible attitude that what cannot be cured must be endured, that one is better off if one is cheerful than if one complains, and that if one gets on with it and keeps doing what one is supposed to be doing, things are likely to work out satisfactorily in the end.

There were, indeed, times when I wondered whether he was imbued with the homely philosophy of Poor Richard or with that of some Stoic sage, but as it turned out, it was not a talent for philosophy that accounted for his attitude and behavior. It was the grim reality of a childhood event that was responsible.

At the age of nine years, the patient had been suddenly threatened with the prospect of being deserted by the person who was to him the most important adult member of his family. For three days, he was acutely and profoundly depressed. Then, fortunately, the danger of being deserted passed. But never permanently, as far as he was concerned. The possibility of abandonment remained ever present in his mind. He reacted to it in two different, logically inconsistent but easily understandable ways. One was to assure, by his behavior, that it would never happen. The other was to prepare himself for the time when it would inevitably happen, so that he would not be helpless and overwhelmed when it finally did.

Before the threatened loss, the patient had been a hot-tempered boy with occasional temper tantrums. Never again. From that time until the time he entered analysis, he could recall but one occasion when he felt really angry. His sexual activities were also curtailed, though by no means as drastically. He became a very good boy, in other words, one who no longer showed the faults of sexual and aggressive behavior, which he had been sure had occasioned the threat of desertion he experienced at age nine. At the same time, he identified with the adult whose loss he had feared. He became, like that adult, cheerful, sensible, practical, and optimistic in an unquestioning sort of way, and practiced taking care of himself as though to say, "I'll never need *that* person again."

In the further course of the patient's analysis, it was learned that the episode just described, when the patient was nine, was not the first of its kind. When he was four, a baby sister was born, who quickly became their mother's favorite child. In other words, what happened when he was nine had such far-reaching consequences because it so closely resembled an earlier conflict situation.

A fourth illustrative example, this time having to do with an avocational choice, is that of a patient in her thirties who had a considerable interest in music. She was well educated musically, for an amateur, and had studied and enjoyed playing a musical instrument without, however, achieving great proficiency. At the time the patient entered analysis, her interest in music was a pleasurable part of her life, and it was often mentioned incidentally early in analysis. Her interest in music was not one of the problems that had brought her to analysis, and she paid it correspondingly little attention. She had grown up in a family in which music was important, and it seemed to her natural that she should be interested in it. The evidence that her interest in music was a compromise formation emerged unexpectedly in connection with a dream.

She dreamed she was playing in an orchestra. Her associations led to memories of a musician with whom she had been in love some years before and who, she had recently heard, had become the conductor of a well-known orchestra. She volunteered the information that he used to remind her of her father, although he was unlike her father both in age and in appearance. Perhaps, she said, it was because both used the same after-shave lotion. She went on to recall that her interest in music as a child was a conscious imitation of her older sister, a woman who was an accomplished professional musician at the time of the patient's dream. Their father prized his older daughter's musical ability and achievements very highly. As a child, it seemed to the patient that her sister was their father's favorite because of her musical talent. The patient herself studied music in imitation of her sister, with the hope of rivaling her in his affections.

Thus, throughout her life, my patient's interest in music and in musicians was simultaneously an expression of her libidinal wishes toward her father and of her admiring and envious, competitive wishes toward her sister. At the same time, it served a defensive function: she never consciously thought of competing with her sister musically in later childhood and adult life. As far as the patient was consciously aware, music was merely an avocation, a source of amusement and pleasure, not a way of being the one and only woman in her father's life.

What I have tried to illustrate is that it is not only the ordinary, normal slips and errors of daily life that prove on analysis to be compromise formations. The same is true for normal character traits, for vocational choice, for hobbies/avocations and, indeed, for any other aspect of mental functioning of the sort that is conventionally and deservedly labeled *normal*. Whenever any normal mental activity can be analyzed in the course of treatment, it is found to be a compromise formation of childhood origin.

Still, the number of examples that can be drawn from analysis to support the idea that conflict is ubiquitous (= normal) is small. Analysis is aimed mainly at understanding mental activity conventionally labeled *abnormal* or *pathological*. What is the evidence from other sources that support the conclusion that compromise formation is the ubiquitous norm?

Works of fiction are one source. To begin with, think of the fairy tales and folk tales that have wide appeal among older children in our society. They are ready-made fantasies that offer to older children the pleasure of the imaginary gratification of the sexual and aggressive wishes of earlier childhood in somewhat disguised form. They are true compromise formations containing also fantasies of calamities that are attendant on those wishes, of anxiety, of depressive affect, and of defense. One of the defenses common to all such stories, in fact, is the premise that they happened long ago, that the actors are strangers, not the reader or listener, and that the story is "just make-believe," not real. Two well-known examples will suffice to make my point.

In the story of Cinderella, a younger sister outshines her mother and older sisters and marries a prince who loves only her, despite the efforts of mother and sisters to prevent it. The story explicitly sets out to satisfy the sexual and aggressive wishes of little girls who are jealous of mother and sisters and who wish father to love them best. At the same time, however, both misery and anxiety figure largely in the plot. Cinderella, as her name indicates, is languishing in misery, clad in rags, and treated like a servant by her rivals until the very end of the story. In addition, there is great anxiety about being punished for her disobedience, thoughtless and unintentional though it is made out to be, as midnight approaches and she continues to enjoy the favors and attention of the prince. There is also a good mother in the form of the fairy godmother, whom Cinderella loves and who loves Cinderella in return. So much so that it is she who helps Cinderella win the prince's love. In short, the contributions of childhood's sexual and aggressive wishes, anxiety and depressive affect, and defense are as evident as such things can be without actual analytic data.

The same is true for the perennially popular British folk tale called "Jack and the Beanstalk." It tells of a boy who robs a giant—a huge man, much larger and stronger than Jack—of his possessions, and then kills the giant by chopping down a beanstalk. The most obvious childhood sexual and aggressive wishes that this story satisfies in the fantasies of its child readers are envy, the desire to have sole possession of mother, castration, and parricide. Fear of retributive destruction by the giant, who is repeatedly about to kill Jack by eating him, is a prominent part of the story, though misery is by no means absent, since at the start of the story, Jack and his mother are poor and faced with starvation. As for defense, the giant in the story is a stranger, not Jack's father. Indeed, in some versions of the story, the giant had murdered

Jack's father and stolen his possessions, so that Jack appears as an avenger of his father's murder, rather than as having committed parricide himself.

And so it goes from one tale to the next. They are ready-made compromise formations that offer children the pleasure of imaginary gratification of their libidinal and aggressive wishes, blended with anxiety and depressive affect and with defense. No story of this sort is equally popular with every child, nor does any include the entire gamut of the pleasure-seeking sexual and aggressive wishes that go to make up any one child's early conflicts. Taken as a whole, however, their number and popularity lend strong support to the conclusion that the conflicts and compromise formations that characterize the ages from three to six continue to be active in normal mental functioning during later childhood. They do not simply disappear or become unimportant.

Another source of support for this conclusion comes from the myths and legends current and important to adults in every society. The myths that adults share are sufficiently similar to one another and to the conflicts and compromise formations of early childhood to justify that statement, as some examples will show. Before I present those examples, however, it should be noted that there are differences as well as similarities between folk tales and myths or legends. Folk tales and fairy stories are for amusement. Myths have a more serious purpose. They profess to explain the origin of a people or tribe, they attempt to explain the nature and origin of men's occupations and of their environment, and/or they are attempts at cosmology. In short, they deal with serious, realistic problems that are of grave concern to the members of the community who share them. In a very real sense, as has been observed more than once, myths are also precursors of scientific theories. They offer answers to the same questions concerning the universe that scientific theories propose to answer. Nevertheless, their relation to psychic conflict is direct and intimate.

The Homeric version of the Greek religious myths is well known. It portrays gods and goddesses as a large family living in a palace on a mountaintop with a father, Zeus; a mother, Hera; and many children. Incest, jealousy, fighting, and intrigue are as common on Homer's Olympus as they are in the mind of any three- to six-year-old child. Murder, however, is impossible. The Homeric gods are immortal and, since Zeus is the strongest, he is always the victor or the final arbiter. The Homeric myth precludes parricide. It never ends in tragedy for the father.

In other religious myths, however, including many Greek ones, the theme of parricide appears directly. The father god meets the same fate as the giant in "Jack and the Beanstalk." He is killed, castrated, and/or eaten by his children, frequently with their mother's help. The children usurp his power and sexual prerogatives only to be destroyed in turn by their own offspring.

In the equally well-known legend of Oedipus, dramatized by Sophocles in the fifth century B.C., the hero slew his father, became king in his place, married his mother, and was, eventually, punished by being blinded and by being cast out of his city to wander the earth as a beggar.

To the Greeks of two or three thousand years ago, these narratives were matters of fact. Looked at today by nonbelievers, they support the conclusion that in the minds of the adult Greeks of antiquity compromise formations arising from conflicts over the sexual and aggressive wishes characteristic of early childhood played a major role in determining thought and behavior. But the articles of religious faith of one society are the myths and superstitions of another, whether the two societies are separated by millennia or whether they are contemporaneous. There is no reason to doubt that this is as true of our own society as of every other. One would expect that its religious beliefs, so important in determining the thought and behavior of its members, also give evidence of being compromise formations arising from conflict over the sexual and aggressive wishes of early childhood.

The Judeo-Christian-Moslem monotheistic religion is dominant in much of the world today. One of its most important tenets is contained in the story of Adam and Eve. According to the Bible the two of them, beloved by God, the father, lived in Eden, a paradise where sex was not permitted and aggression/murder did not exist. But only on condition that they refrain from sexual intercourse. As soon as they engaged with one another sexually, which God had expressly forbidden them to do, God no longer loved them. They were expelled from paradise, were forced to support themselves, and no longer lived forever. They, and for that matter all their descendants, suffered God's/father's disapproval and punishment. Again, evidence that supports the conclusion that the conflicts over childhood sexual and aggressive wishes are active in the minds of adults and are important determinants of normal thought and behavior.

Another tenet that speaks for the same conclusion is the belief, held by Jews and Moslems, that the penises of male children should be mutilated by circumcision in infancy or early childhood. The Jewish belief is that God made a covenant (= brith) with Abraham that God would love and protect only the circumcised. They would be his chosen people. Here again is evidence that mental functioning in adults is normally governed by compromise formations of childhood origin. Even Jews and Moslems who consciously reject the beliefs and practices of their respective religions are loath to forgo circumcision of their male offspring. The practice, based as it is on the fantasies of early childhood concerning retribution for sexual and aggressive wishes, persists, however it may be rationalized.

Two other illustrative examples have to do with Moses and with Jesus. It is neither possible nor necessary for me to survey the story of either completely. My discussion will be based on a few of the principal elements of each.

Moses, supposedly born a Jew, was reared as a prince in the Egyptian court. In time, he rebelled against the king, defeated him, caused him to die, and became himself a king with a people and a country of his own. By contrast, in his attitude toward his other father, God, Moses was loving and obedient. He is depicted as serving God faithfully and as punishing those who would rebel against him by worshipping other gods, i.e., as punishing those who would kill Moses's God and replace him with another. In short, the legendary Moses was thoroughly identified with God and submissive to him. In turn, according to pious Jewish belief, God customarily addressed Moses as his son.

By thus giving Moses two fathers, the Moses narrative disguises the theme of parricide. According to it Moses is not to be blamed for getting rid of the Egyptian king. It was the king who was bad; it was he who disobeyed God; it was God who decided to get rid of the king; and, besides, the king was not Moses's real father. Moses was really a Jew, not an Egyptian prince. Thus, according to the biblical text, Moses was not a parricide, but his heavenly father's faithful, loving, obedient son. True, he is said to have disobeyed God in a minor way, for which disobedience God punished him by refusing to let him enter his promised homeland, but the main message of the story is how faithful and obedient Moses was to his Jewish father, and that the Egyptian father who was killed, along with thousands of other Egyptians, deserved to be killed: he wasn't really Moses's father, and anyway he was killed by Moses's other father, God, and not by Moses at all.

As a myth, therefore, the story of Moses, an article of religious belief for current, monotheistic society, supports the conclusion that the conflicts and compromise formations of childhood (in this case, ones concerned mainly with parricide) continue to be active in the minds of adults and play a major role in determining their thoughts and feelings.

The same is true of the story of Jesus. As in the Moses story, the principal and explicit emphasis is on the love of son for father. Jesus and his father, God, are represented as so closely identified that they are actually one and the same. Jesus never rebels. On the contrary, he is so obedient to his father's will that he permits his father to have him killed, after which son and father are lovingly united forever. The theme of parricide appears in the story only implicitly, but it is there, nevertheless. According to the story it is not the hero who is a parricide either in wish or deed. It is bad men, Romans and Jews, who crucify the young Jesus, who is also, in the story, God the father. It is they, not he, who commit parricide. Jesus is their victim instead of their leader.

The theme of conflict over sexual wishes is even less prominent in the legend. It appears incidentally, as a mere hint. According to the story, Jesus came to earth and God had him killed in order to redeem mankind from original sin, which God would otherwise punish implacably. And, as every true believer knows, man's original sin was the sin of Adam and Eve in the Garden of Eden. Jesus was killed by God to expiate the sin of having sexual intercourse against the father-God's express command, though the narrative does not say so in so many words.

Another source of support for the thesis that conflicts and compromise formation of childhood origin are active in the minds of all adults comes from popular literature for adults. Daily newspapers feature true-life stories and pictures of sexual behavior and of violence because those are what interest their adult readers. Bestsellers and pulp fiction are full of manufactured stories dealing with the same themes. Incest has a perennial appeal for adults, as does murder, just as much as they have for children. Defense is equally prominent in these recreational activities. The true-life stories are greeted with conscious disapproval, disgust, or horror. The fictional ones are, after all, only make-believe. Besides, "everyone" reads them. Reading them is not a sign that the *reader* would ever like to do the dreadful things that people do in the stories.

Truly great works of fiction must fulfill requirements of form, but their content is often as revealing as that of pulp fiction. Take *Anna Karenina*, for example, which is surely among the greatest novels ever written. It is, in briefest brief, the story of a young woman who leaves her son and her much older husband because she is in love with another man, and who then proceeds to alienate her lover and, after many months of anguish, to kill herself. The reader is distracted and charmed by the skill of the narrator, but the content of the story is as transparent as that of any fairy tale.

When murder is made a social duty, as it is when a society is at war, adults engage in it with enthusiasm. It is the ones who raise objections who meet with disapproval. And those engaged in killing others also feel freer to be sexually aggressive. And something similar is apparent in certain institutionalized holidays, like the Roman Saturnalia and the current Mardi Gras, followed by days of fasting.

Jokes and humor are another source of supportive evidence. In our society, children take open pleasure in bathroom and toilet activities, and exhibit great interest in such activities of others. Their interest is part of what Freud (1905) called *infantile sexuality*. Normally in our society adults exhibit disinterest and/or disgust with such thoughts and actions. Yet one can witness the spectacle of a thousand adults who have each paid a substantial sum of money for the pleasure of listening to a popular comedian talk about defecation and urination. Scatological stories are perennially popular, as everyone knows who aspires to be an entertaining storyteller to adults.

My point is that there is much nonanalytic evidence that supports the conclusion that conflict and compromise formation resulting from the sexual and aggressive wishes of early childhood persist throughout life and are important determinants of thought and action at least as long as the brain is functionally intact. To say, for example, that all religious believers throughout history are and have been mentally abnormal undermines the very meaning of the word. What one can say, on the basis of the relevant evidence, is that the sexual and aggressive wishes of ages three to six invariably give rise to conflicts and compromise formation that determine each person's thoughts and actions to a major extent for the rest of their lives. They remain active in the minds of all forever after. They are not signs of psychopathology. They are ubiquitous (Brenner 1982).

In line with this realization comes a concept of psychopathology that is based simply on quantitative considerations. This is a concept that is of such great importance in modern conflict theory that I italicize it for emphasis. *If a person's compromise formations allow for an adequate degree of pleasurable gratification of childhood sexual and aggressive wishes, if they don't involve too much unpleasure in the form of anxiety and depressive affect, and if there is not too much defensive inhibition of function and too great a need for self-punishment and self-injury, then the person in question should be considered mentally normal or well. If the contrary is the case, if there is too little gratification of childhood pleasure-seeking wishes, too much unpleasure, and too much inhibition of function and too much self-injury, that person is to be considered mentally ill or abnormal.* The decision whether to call someone mentally ill or mentally well must always be a matter of just such judgment.

It follows from this concept of psychopathology that the aim of psychoanalysis must be to alter a patient's compromise formations from the so-called pathological to the so-called normal. The childhood sexual and aggressive wishes and the conflicts associated with them never disappear. It is only the compromise formations to which they give rise that can change. What remains, then, is to describe the method by which a pathological compromise formation becomes a normal one.

CHAPTER 4

Let me preface my exposition by saying that, in my opinion, any written account of it will inevitably leave much to be desired (Brenner 1976, pp. 5-7). The ideal way to learn how someone analyzes would be to watch and listen to her/him do it. To be the third party in the room with an analyst and patient, however, is clearly not possible. Even to observe through a one-way mirror or to listen to audiotape recordings would involve so much time and attention over so long a period as to be essentially out of the question. The best way that's practical is for the would-be observer to discuss a case of her/his own at frequent, regular intervals, something that analysts usually do as part of their analytic education. When one is faced with an audience of readers, however, instead of a single colleague, all one can do is to enunciate principles of general application and enrich them with clinical vignettes. It is simply not possible to give a full view of the treatment of any single case in printed form. Nobody would have the patience to write it and, by the same token, no one would have the interest and patience to read it. With this caveat, I shall proceed.

The Aim of Psychoanalysis

What, to start with, is the aim—the goal—of analysis? Since it is an integral part of modern conflict theory that conflicts and compromise formations resulting from the sexual and aggressive wishes of childhood are both normal and ubiquitous and, furthermore, that they persist throughout life, it follows that they are never *resolved* by analysis. The aim of analysis is not the resolution or disappearance of the conflicts responsible for the compromise formations called neurotic symptoms and neurotic character traits. Such an aim is an illusory, an impossible one. The aim of analysis can only be to *alter* a patient's pathological compromise formations. It can never be to eliminate them or the conflicts from which they arise. As I noted earlier, the difference between a normal compromise formation and a pathological one is simply this. If the compromise formation(s) allow for an adequate degree of pleasurable satisfaction of sexual and aggressive wishes of childhood origin, if they don't involve too much unpleasure in the form of anxiety and depressive affect, if their defenses don't involve too much inhibition of function and too much in the way of self-injury and self-punishment, they are rightly viewed as normal. If not, they are rightly viewed as pathological. What psychoanalysis can accomplish, when it is successful, is to permit more pleasurable gratification, to diminish the associated unpleasure, and to involve less inhibition and less self-punishment. And, be it noted, these are not minor achievements. They can mean the difference between illness, even fatal illness, and health. But the childhood wishes and the conflicts to which they have given rise never disappear. It is only their consequences, the resultant compromise formations, that change. A successful analysis can change them. It can never make the childhood wishes and compromise formations disappear.

Termination

If this is so, how is one able to decide that a patient's analysis is over? In the past, the formula most often used was that an analysis is complete when a patient's conflicts have been resolved. If in fact they are never resolved, i.e., if they never disappear, does that mean that no analysis can ever be considered completed?

To be sure, as a practical matter, a patient may feel sufficiently improved symptomatically so that she/he declares there is no need for further treatment, and often in such a case the analyst may agree. But there are certainly times, perhaps times in every analysis, when a patient wants to stop analysis and the analyst has good reason to believe that for the patient to stop would be very much against the patient's best interest, and that the wish to stop should be analyzed rather than agreed to. How to decide?

In trying to reach a decision in such a case, the question an analyst must always have in mind is "Have the previous pathological compromise formations been sufficiently altered or not?" If, in the analyst's opinion, they have been, it's time to stop. If not, the analyst's recommendation will be that analysis should continue unless, of course, the analyst has come to the conclusion that he or she is unable to help the patient further. The decision is always a matter of clinical judgment. It can be nothing else. There is no sharp line, no qualitative difference, between normality and pathology in mental functioning. The distinction can only be based on clinical judgment. And one thing is clear: conflicts are never "resolved."

I should add that if an analyst feels that analysis is at a standstill despite her/his best efforts, my advice is that the best thing to do is to present the case to a colleague and to discuss the problem(s) involved. Indeed, it has even happened on occasion that an analyst, on reviewing a case in order to present it to me, came to the beginning of a better understanding of how to deal with the problem on his/her own before ever discussing it with me. Which suggests that reviewing one's cases to oneself periodically is also likely to be helpful, even when they seem to be going satisfactorily.

Description of Psychoanalytic Technique

How should one describe the method by which an analyst attempts to achieve the goal just described? What are the essentials, in my opinion, of a proper psychoanalytic technique?

I say *in my opinion* because there is as much disagreement among analysts about the specifics of psychoanalytic technique, as there is about theories of how the mind develops and functions. All are agreed that an analyst listens while the patient talks and then intervenes at what is considered to be an appropriate time, but there agreement ends. Some analysts emphasize that, right from the start, one must take steps to create a dependable working relationship with a patient if analysis is to succeed. Some rely on the spontaneous development of a so-called psychoanalytic process that they believe to be more or less independent of the content of the analyst's interventions. Some recommend that interpretive interventions be restricted to explicating or demonstrating defenses. Some deny the value of paying any attention to defenses. Some try to establish a so-called holding environment. Some try to explain to patients how their minds work. Others decry the value of such explanations. Some rely on intuition, some on countertransference. Some maintain that only interpretations of the transference produce any genuine insight and improvement. Some define analysis by the patient's position: sitting up is not analysis; lying on a couch is analysis. The list is doubtless incomplete, but it is long enough to make evident that there is no consensus among analysts about the principles of psychoanalytic technique.

Analytic Attitude

My own opinion is that, in doing analysis, what is essential is that the analyst adopt and maintain an analytic attitude. An analyst should always be trying to understand. If one were to try to describe a proper analytic attitude by a single word, the word would be "Why?" Why did this thought follow that? Why this emotional expression just now? Why did the patient act in just this way outside the analytic situation? Why this or that behavior in the past? Why these plans, or lack of them, for the future? And, always, why this response to what the analyst just said or to the analyst's silence?

Whatever a patient says or does, the analyst's attitude should be one of curiosity about the words and actions. It is not an analyst's place to approve or disapprove, to encourage or discourage, to be seductive or the reverse. To behave in any of those ways will interfere with the analytic work or even render it impossible. *Neutral* is the word often used to describe this aspect of the analytic attitude. It is an apt word in some respects, but not in all. In one important respect at least an analyst should be anything but neutral. Analysis is a therapeutic undertaking and an analyst's intent should not be to be as "neutral" as possible, but to be as *good* a therapist as possible. My point is that, in analysis, to be as good a therapist as possible is to be consistently analytic—to maintain an analytic attitude, i.e., to try at all times to understand one's patients and, by conveying that understanding to them to help them be able to change their compromise formations for the better.

A good example of what I mean is the often vexing problem of what to do when a patient asks a direct question. It is obvious that some questions must be answered sooner or later—questions of scheduling and the like. Often, however, it is to a patient's advantage that the patient think and talk about having asked the question (= to "associate") instead of having it answered. Even when the question is one that must be answered (e.g., scheduling), it is potentially useful to inquire for the patient's thoughts about it. Everything, not just some things, but *everything* is potentially a useful source of information about a patient's conflicts and compromise formations. An analyst's attitude should always be, "Why?" It is always in the best interest of the patient for it to be so and every patient should be so informed to make sure that he or she understands that when an analyst doesn't answer a question it is because the analyst believes it to be in the patient's interest that the analyst not do so. To ask for a patient's associations (= thoughts) instead of answering a question is not being "depriving," "rigid," or "doctrinaire" in a pejorative sense. On the contrary, it is an attempt, often a successful attempt, to be as helpful as possible.

To repeat, in the course of analytic work, an analyst is engaged in forming conjectures, in communicating them as interpretations, and in observing the patient's response to whatever interpretations are offered. Even in such extreme cases, which are by no means rare, as when a patient refuses to speak, or refuses to speak about certain topics, or refuses to listen to what the analyst says or distorts or misunderstands it, the analyst does best not by attempting to exert authority, however benevolently, but by attempting to understand and to interpret. What is best for an analyst to do in analysis is to analyze. Just as it is presumptuous to act the analyst unbidden in a social situation other than analysis, so it is a technical lapse to be other than an analyst in one's relation with an analytic patient. In every instance, what one says or does should be determined by one's attitude of concern to learn as much as possible of the nature and origins of each patient's conflicts, in order to help the patient do the same.

Authority

How to deal with direct questions is part of the more general problem of an analyst's "authority." My opinion on the subject of authority is this. Analysis is not an exercise in egalitarianism or, as many prefer to call it, in democracy. Every therapist, whether analyst or not, has and must exercise some degree of authority. An analyst's exercise of authority is but a special case of that general rule (Brenner 1995). When an analyst suggests to a patient that the patient lie on a couch and speak freely, the analyst is exerting authority based on the analyst's knowledge of psychodynamics and on the analyst's understanding of the proper technique of analysis. Some appeal to knowledge and the exercise of some degree of authority are essential parts of the relationship between analyst and patient, just as they are between therapist and patient in any therapeutic situation. To put the matter simply, it is the exercise of an appropriate degree of professional authority for an analyst to convey to a patient that the thing to do, in order to obtain relief, is to talk as freely as possible and to listen to what the analyst has to say when the analyst speaks. I believe it is inappropriate and unanalytic for an analyst to take the position that each patient knows best what sort of treatment is appropriate and to totally defer to a patient's ideas about how therapy should be conducted. As I said earlier, analysis is not an exercise in "democracy."

Granted that authority plays a role at least to the extent just indicated, there is real question about the exercise of authority by an analyst during the course of analysis. Analysts often correctly think they know what is going on in a patient's mind better than the patient does. Should an analyst ever say this to a patient? Should a patient even glean from the analyst's manner and mode of speech that the analyst believes this to be the case? Should analysts ever, on the basis of presumed better knowledge, set themselves up as authorities or, still worse, be seen as authoritarian?

I believe that in attempting to answer these questions, one should be guided by what was said in the first chapter about the nature of truth in any scientific discipline. An analyst's opinion about what is going on in a patient's mind is the best conclusion the analyst can draw from the available, relevant evidence. No matter how certain an analyst is that a conjecture of this sort is a valid one, it is inappropriate to present it to a patient as anything but a conjecture. To be authoritarian, insistent, or even argumentative with a patient, it seems to me, is simply unanalytic. Which is not to say that there is anything unanalytic, in principle, about making clear to a patient that one believes that a particular conjecture is a valid one, whether the patient agrees with it or not. Whether one does so or not will depend on whether one thinks such a statement is likely to be helpful in forwarding the work of analysis, but there is no reason for not disclosing to a patient what one's opinion is about what is going on in the patient's mind if one thinks it will be helpful to do so.

The following example will illustrate what I mean. A young woman, thirty years old, complained that she couldn't have a satisfactory relationship with a man. She was living with her divorced father, and it gradually emerged that she had backed out of two perfectly suitable arrangements to leave him and to share an apartment with a woman friend, something that would have greatly improved the likelihood of her getting to know more men of her own age. The patient's expressed wish was to leave her father, to live independently, and to meet men. She maintained that her only reasons for staying with her father were, first, that he wanted her to and, second, that she would feel guilty about leaving him, because then he would be all alone. I believe it was analytically appropriate and helpful for her analyst to say to the patient that, in the analyst's opinion, she had reasons for staying with her father in addition to the ones she consciously acknowledged.

It should be noted in this connection that there are at least two reasons why a knowledgeable, experienced analyst is in a much better position to understand the nature and origins of a patient's conflicts than the patient is. One is that the analyst usually knows more than the patient does about how people's minds work. The other is implicit in the analytic situation. Patients, like all mankind, are engaged in deceiving themselves about some of their most powerful motives. Defense is an essential part of conflict, and self-deception is the essence of defense. In most instances, therefore, conjectures of analysts, who have less need to deceive themselves about a patient's conflicts than the patient does, are more likely to be accurate. It is always possible to be mistaken or to overlook something, but when analyst and patient differ, the patient is not likely to be a reliable court of last resort. One should always listen with attention to what a patient has to say, but not with the idea that the patient is a reliable arbiter. If an analyst should have serious doubt about the correctness of a conjecture, a consultation with a colleague is much more likely to be helpful than a misguided deference to the patient as a presumed peer.

To be sure every analyst is a participant observer with his or her own conflicts and compromise formations of childhood origin and these will necessarily influence an analyst's observations and conclusions. But the question is not whether an analyst's own conflicts influence the analyst's conjectures and the patient's associations, which constitute the data on which conjectures are based; I believe that there is no doubt that they do, always, as they always do in every field of scientific endeavor. The question in each individual case is whether the influence referred to is such that it interferes with the observations made and the conjectures one hopes to be able to draw from them, to such an extent as to make those conjectures unreliable. I believe that, in a properly conducted analysis, the analyst's effect on the data is not so great as to render them unreliable for the purpose to which one hopes to put them, i.e., as a basis for understanding the nature and origin of a patient's conflicts and, by extension, as a basis for conveying that understanding to a patient.

The way in which one does convey one's understanding to a patient deserves some consideration here. There are no prescriptions about phrasing, about tone of voice, about the use of metaphor or humor that fit every situation. It is the analyst's attitude that is of fundamental importance in the timing of interpretations and in the way in which they are presented, as is the case with every other aspect of the analytic endeavor. In making an interpretation, an analyst is in the position of trying to explain to another person, the patient, what the analyst thinks might be motivating the patient, even though the patient is trying to hide the fact, in one way or another, from her- or himself. When one is trying to explain something to another person, one may talk more softly at one time, more loudly at another, more hesitantly now, with more certainty then, and so on. One may be persuasive at times, factual at times, humorous at times, as the situation warrants and as one happens to feel. What one should not be in an analytic situation is either angry, arrogant, and disapproving, on the one hand, or seductive or disingenuous on the other. An analyst's attitude should be that of one who tries to understand and then to explain, hoping that the explanations offered are both correct and helpful, but one whose chief interest beyond those considerations is not in convincing the patient, but in observing and trying to understand the patient's reaction to whatever interpretation has been made.

The Criteria of an Analytic Situation

It should be clear from this discussion that, in my opinion, an analytic situation cannot be created simply by applying rules of thumb or simply by making certain physical arrangements. The physical arrangements are merely adjuvants to the task of speaking as freely and frankly as possible. Patients are seen in a quiet room, relatively free from intrusion and disturbances of sight, sound, and smell, for the obvious reason that it's easier for most people to reveal their wishes, fears, miseries, and guilt if they aren't distracted by intrusive noises, lights, or odors. For very similar reasons, patients are advised to lie on a couch that is comfortable and relaxing—not that they necessarily are relaxed, but at least they're in a position in which they can relax. One learns more that's useful if a patient's movements and muscular tension are the result of their own conflicts than if they are stimulated or set in motion by being placed in a physically uncomfortable position. To look at and be looked at by the therapist is also an unnecessary, distracting stimulus, and it is for that reason that the analyst's position is out of range of the patient's vision.

It is obvious that all these arrangements are not essential to analysis. They are merely aids to the process. The walls of one's office need not be bare. A patient's reaction to a picture on the wall, or to its absence, may reveal useful information about the patient's conflicts. The same is true for reactions to the analyst's clothes, manner of greeting or of leave taking, tone of voice, and so on. There is nothing magical about having the analyst out of range of the patient's vision, for example. It's just that such an arrangement is, by and large, helpful to the work of analysis. The same is true of using the couch. Why wouldn't an easy chair for the patient do just as well? My answer is that I'm sure it would. In at least one of the photographs of Freud's couch, one can see that his patients had so many cushions behind them that they were very nearly in a sitting position when they were on his couch. And he himself referred to the patient's supine position as being merely a holdover from the hypnotic method of treatment that he used before he developed the now-familiar analytic one. The choice of a couch rather than an easy chair is obligatory today only because a couch is traditional, and an easy chair would be an innovation. Nearly every patient who comes for analysis today expects to use a couch. To recommend a chair instead would uselessly complicate the analytic situation and stir up questions in the patient's mind at a time and in a way that I think would be undesirable. What one tries to do with these practical aspects of the analytic situation is simply to arrange things so as to offer what one hopes will be optimal conditions for the patient's talking freely.

We assume, correctly I think, that most patients will talk more freely if they're in a room with closed doors than they will if people are wandering in and out all the time. But we assume, also correctly, that the analyst's promise that what a patient says will be kept confidential is even more important than any of the physical arrangements I have been talking about. Whatever physical and other arrangements seem likely to be helpful in getting a patient to talk more freely are what one should provide.

Similar considerations apply to the question of frequency of visits. There is nothing magical about five sessions a week as compared with two or three. One can do analytic work on the less intensive schedule. The point is simply that one can do more and better analytic work on a more intensive schedule than on a less intensive one. Two or three times a week isn't "bad" or unanalytic. It's just working under a handicap as compared with four or five times a week. Anyone who has experimented with both knows that the more frequent schedule provides a much better sense of continuity and a much better understanding of a patient's mental functioning from day to day than does the less frequent schedule. If a patient who can come more frequently prefers or insists on coming less often, that is something to be analyzed, not something to go along with without question.

What about charging for missed sessions? Should one charge for all missed sessions or should one not charge if a session is missed for reasons beyond a patient's control? Or should one, perhaps, offer make-up sessions? Should one charge if a patient takes a holiday at a time when the analyst is working?

It seems to me that the issues revolving around payment are basically different in one important respect from the question of other practical arrangements. Patients are not asked to pay because paying makes it easier for them to talk freely. Patients are asked to pay because analysts earn their living that way. Paying is, in the first instance, something the analyst wants for his or her own reasons, not because it benefits a patient's analysis. To be sure, this is a statement that should be amended and expanded. Depending on a patient's fantasies about the fee, paying or not paying can be of great importance to an understanding of a patient's conflicts. And for a particular patient to pay or not pay under particular circumstances may very much affect a patient's ability to talk freely, as every analyst knows. All I mean to say is that the fundamental, the most important reason for paying is for the analyst to earn a living. In general, whatever arrangements an analyst decides to make about paying represent what that analyst prefers. Provided the arrangements are reasonable ones and within generally accepted, conventional limits, they should not present any important obstacle to analysis. A patient's reaction to them should be analyzed if the reaction appears as a significant part of the analytic material, but both patient and analyst should know that financial arrangements are, in the last analysis, decided by the analyst's preference. They're not something that's put forward by the analyst because they're to a patient's advantage.

The "Fundamental Rule" of Analysis

The counterpart of the analyst's attitude is the patient's task of reporting as freely as possible all conscious thoughts and feelings (= the "fundamental rule"). It is this report that is the main source of data for an analyst's conclusions about the nature and origins of a patient's conflicts. Any difficulty that a patient experiences or demonstrates in the effort to conform to that task is an expression of a compromise formation that, in principle, deserves to be analyzed. An analyst notes a patient's silence or sleepiness or avoidance of important topics or any other evidence of difficulty in speaking freely, calls the patient's attention to it when it seems important to do so, and asks for the patient's thoughts about it. What a patient is able to say about the matter will reveal something about the defenses, about the nature of the childhood calamities, and about the sexual and aggressive wishes of childhood origin that are the elements of the conflict underlying the difficulty. One can expect that every patient will have difficulties of this sort from time to time. If it were not so, there would be no need for analysis in the first place, if our understanding of mental functioning is correct. "Psychological mindedness" and "an ability to free associate" are not to be thought of as attributes that indicate whether a patient is likely to be helped by psychoanalysis. Difficulties in speaking freely are something to analyze. They are not unalterable character traits. And the same for psychological mindedness. A patient's psychological obtuseness, like everything else, is a compromise formation, something analyzable in principle. When confronted with either of these difficulties on the part of a patient, the analyst should ask, "Why?" "Why a lack of interest about what goes on in her/his or other people's minds? Why a difficulty in speaking freely just now, or about this particular topic?"

Transference

I think it's fair to say that all analysts will agree that one of the important aspects of mental life both in childhood and in adulthood is what are called object relations, i.e., one's relations with the other persons in one's life. And according to modern conflict theory, every thought and every action having to do with another person in one's life is determinatively influenced by the conflicts and compromise formations resulting from the sexual and aggressive wishes of early life. Every one is a compromise formation.

In the analytic situation, as all analysts know, a patient's thoughts and feelings about the analyst are of great practical importance. So much so that they are given a special name, *transference*, and in his early papers on technique Freud rightly emphasized the special importance that transference has in every analytic situation. Its importance has at times led to the conclusion that there is something special about transference, in the sense that it is unique to the analytic situation. It is not. What is called transference is ubiquitous. What is unique about patients' thoughts about the analyst in every analysis is not their appearance. It is the fact that they are analyzed rather than responded to in any of the usual, socially conventional ways.

In fact a better understanding of transference is another example of the value of modern conflict theory. It enables one to answer satisfactorily a number of previously puzzling questions. Is it true, for example, that a "true transference neurosis" must develop if an analysis is to qualify as genuine? Again, what is meant by the terms "erotized transference" and/or "highly erotic transference"? For another, how does one deal with a negative transference? And how about "benign positive transference"? What is meant by transference regression? Is "regression in the transference" a hallmark of analytic therapy? And, finally, how about patients who never develop a transference?

To take the last question first, modern conflict theory makes clear that it is an oxymoron. Whatever patients think and feel about their analyst is a compromise formation. This is as true for a patient who is aware only of indifference as it is for one who is aware of strong feelings toward the analyst. According to modern conflict theory, that's the way the mind works. Whatever a patient's thoughts and feelings about his or her analyst may be, they are compromise formations that are determinatively influenced by conflicts over childhood sexual and aggressive wishes. There can never be *no* transference. Every relation with another person is "transferred" from childhood. The compromise formation may take the form of being unaware that there are any feelings at all, but they are there nonetheless—always. Whatever a patient's conscious and unconscious thoughts about the analyst may be, they are always compromise formations arising from childhood conflicts. To say that a patient has no transference is to assert the impossible.

Transference neurosis is a term that by now is hardly definable. It has an interesting history. What it was originally intended to mean is this. At the beginning of an analysis, Freud said, there is (often) a brief honeymoon period during which the patient accepts all the analyst's interpretations and rapidly becomes symptom free. This happens because the patient has unconsciously fallen in love with the analyst and expects the analyst to gratify the patient's childhood sexual wishes, something that the patient's parents had not done in the patient's childhood. When this expectation is frustrated by the analyst's continuing to behave as an analyst and not as a lover, the patient's symptoms all return, only now, instead of the patient's sexual and aggressive wishes being centered on his or her parents, they are centered on the analyst. The patient's original neurosis has become a transference neurosis and must be analyzed as such.

The term has long since lost the original meaning Freud gave it. As far as I can judge from discussions with colleagues, its current meaning is this. In every analysis a patient's thoughts and feelings about the analyst must be analyzed. Analysis of the transference is a part of every analysis. If those thoughts and feelings can be successfully analyzed, they are called a *transference neurosis*. If not, the label given them is *resistance* or *unanalyzable transference*. In other words, what the term *transference neurosis* most often means at present, as far as I can judge, is *analyzable transference*. If the term is taken seriously, it is simply a tautology, since both *neurosis* and *transference* refer to the same sort of compromise formations.

What about *erotic transferences?* Experience has long since shown that all object relations are ambivalent. Sexual and aggressive wishes characterize them all. To speak of an *erotic transference* is to use a confusing misnomer. Sexual wishes, conscious or not, are part of every object relationship. That of patient to analyst is no exception. One should not speak of an erotic transference as though there were some other kind. Every transference is erotic, just as every one includes aggressive wishes as well.

Nor should one speak of a transference as positive or negative. There is always a mixture of sexual and aggressive wishes. One can speak appropriately of negative or positive feelings that patients have toward their analysts, but no transference is ever simply positive or negative.

Benign positive transference is another concept that deserves to be discarded. What value it originally had has long since vanished. It is at best a poor name for whatever aspects of a patient's thoughts about the analyst help, at the moment, to further the work of analysis. In this connection, one should bear in mind that thoughts and wishes can often be inferred from actions. However antagonistically a patient may be speaking and acting, the fact that he or she is continuing to come to her/his sessions indicates a desire to cooperate.

The idea that transference entails regression, and the related idea that regression necessarily increases as analysis proceeds—that regression is a sign of progress—are also based on a misconception. What happens in the course of a successful analysis is not that a patient's mental functioning becomes more infantile. What happens is that, as the analysis proceeds, the patient becomes more and more able both to tolerate and to understand her/his sexual and aggressive wishes of childhood origin and to obtain pleasure from their satisfaction in one form or another. To say that such wishes and the conflicts to which they give rise are more apparent (= better understood) later in analysis than they are early on is not to say that they become either more frequent or more important as analysis progresses. They are present at every stage of analysis—just as much at the beginning as at the end.

In summary, then, what modern conflict theory does, as far as understanding transference is concerned, is to make clear that what is called *transference* is no different in its origin or in the dynamics of its functioning from any other object relationship. From which the conclusion to be drawn is that, whenever indicated, a patient's thoughts and feelings about the analyst are to be analyzed in just the same way as are any other important and conflict-laden aspects of the patient's life. Like anything else in the analytic material, analysis of thoughts and feelings about the analyst will lead to a fuller understanding of the patient's conflicts of childhood origin.

Countertransference

To turn from the subject of transference to that of countertransference, what is true for patients in analysis is equally true for analysts practicing analysis. An analyst's relation with each patient is also determined, genetically and dynamically, by the analyst's conflicts and compromise formations resulting from the analyst's sexual and aggressive wishes of childhood origin. Analysts, like patients, are human beings. What is called *countertransference* is ubiquitous. In that respect, it is no different from what is called *transference*. The *practical importance* of transference is whether it is analyzable, as has already been said. The *practical importance* of countertransference depends on whether it interferes with the work of analysis or whether it assists the process. The great importance of each in the conduct of every analysis should not mislead one as to their nature and genesis. Both are subheadings under the heading of object relations.

That there are differences as well as similarities between the two is obvious, and it is the differences that account for the fact that each should be treated differently in the course of analysis. A patient's thoughts and feelings about the analyst are to be analyzed, rather than responded to in some other way. It is a way of responding that is unique to analysis. In my opinion, an analyst's thoughts about the patient, however, should not be analyzed in the same way, i.e., with the patient's participation, during the patient's analytic session. The analogue to analysis of a patient's thoughts about the analyst is not analysis of the analyst's thoughts about the patient; it is an analyst's reflections upon and knowledge of his or her conflicts and compromise formations gained from personal analysis. If an analyst acts in a way that is unanalytic—in a way determined by the analyst's conflicts of childhood origin as, for example, in forgetting an appointment—what is most helpful is to discover and to understand the patient's reaction to what the analyst has done or failed to do. To be sure, an analyst should be curious and should try to discover what his or her motives were, but to do so is usually less important for the progress of the analysis than is an understanding of the patient's reaction. If an analyst is in serious difficulty with one or more patients, all would agree that what is indicated is consultation with a colleague for help with whatever is causing the difficulty.

Again, in summary, both transference and countertransference are topics of special importance in any discussion of psychoanalytic technique. They are not phenomena that are unique to the analytic situation, however. Transference and countertransference are subheadings under the aspect of mental functioning that is labeled *object relations*. They are, like every other relationship that one has with the persons with whom one is in contact, compromise formations that stem from conflicts over the sexual and aggressive wishes of childhood. (See Brenner 1982, chapter 12, for a more extensive discussion of both subjects.)

Dreams and Dream Analysis

Another topic of special importance in analytic technique is dreaming. It is fair to say that, in our society, dreams are of no special importance in daily life, but they occupy a place of great importance in psychoanalysis. Just as analysis has been described or defined at times as the form of psychotherapy in which transference appears and is analyzed, it has also been defined at times as the form of therapy in which dreams are interpreted. As every analyst knows, Freud took special pride in *The Interpretation of Dreams* (1900) and, on occasion, called dreams the royal road or, as we might say today, the superhighway to the unconscious.

My own views on this very special subject are these. Dreams are, like all else in mental life, compromise formations. The sexual and aggressive wishes of early childhood play their part in dream formation, as do the associated fears and miseries connected with them and the related defenses and self-punitive trends. If a patient can speak freely enough about the various thoughts and images of a dream, one can learn much about the nature and origins of the patient's compromise formations. In my experience, however, they are not superior in this respect to anything else in mental functioning. Since they are compromise formations, there is always a component of disguise and distortion—of an effort to avoid acknowledgment of the sexual and aggressive wishes that are involved—and, on occasion, as Freud recognized, this component may predominate. Dreams, like anything else, can be roadblocks as well as well-paved roads. When they appear in the course of a patient's associations, they certainly deserve attention, but in my opinion, they do not deserve the special attention that is often given to them. Every psychoanalytic institute with whose curriculum I am familiar has special courses on dream psychology—consisting usually of a thorough study of Freud's masterwork—and it is not rare for there to be a special course on the use of dreams in clinical work. I believe this is not justified. It is a waste of valuable time. A particular dream may be, when analyzed, of great value in the course of an analysis. But the same is true of any other compromise formation, and there is nothing unique or arcane about how one should go about analyzing dreams.

There is nothing new in this, of course. Most analysts understand quite well that not every dream is a potential royal road to the unconscious. Still, there is a tendency to think that there's something magical about some dreams, at least. That when a dream isn't in the service of resistance, its analysis can tell more about a patient's conflicts than can the analysis of anything else a patient may communicate. I believe that this is not the case. Anything a patient says or does, anything in the analytic material, has the same potential, whether it be a nocturnal dream, a daydream, a symptom, a manifestation of transference, or, for that matter, a slip of the tongue, a chance remark, a rush of tears, or a burst of laughter. Everything is a compromise formation that is the result of conflict resulting from childhood sexual and aggressive wishes. Not just dreams. Everything.

Symptom Analysis

There is a long-standing tradition among analysts that one should not try to analyze patients' symptoms. The dictum is that one should analyze patients' conflicts and not their symptoms, and that if one does so, the symptoms will disappear without having been directly addressed. One can only guess at the origin of such a nonsensical recommendation. Perhaps the wise and necessary advice that in analysis it is better not to try to alleviate patients' symptoms by such nonanalytic methods as expressions of sympathy or encouragement gave rise to the idea—anything but wise—

that in analysis symptoms should be ignored altogether. Whatever the reason may be, the fact is that the curriculum of every psychoanalytic institute includes courses on learning about patients' conflicts by analyzing their dreams, by analyzing their transferences, by analyzing their characterological abnormalities, but I know of none addressed to the analysis of patients' symptoms. By emphasizing that symptoms, like everything else in mental life, are compromise formations that result from conflict, modern conflict theory appropriately directs analysts' attention to the value of symptoms as sources of information about patients' conflicts when properly analyzed. The following will serve as an example.

The mind of a young man who had been considering entering analysis for some time was finally made up by the occurrence of a severe, acute attack of anxiety. In telling me about it when he came for a consultation, he explained that at the time of the attack he was in a home appliance store where he was buying some kitchen utensils. He was about to move into an apartment of his own for the first time. Until then he had been living with his grandmother. He went on to explain his somewhat unusual family history. His parents, who had married when his mother was very young, had divorced in his infancy and he had had very little contact with his father, except for financial support. Both he and his mother had lived with his grandmother, who had been the patient's principal maternal caretaker throughout his life. What was unusual was that the patient was passed off as his grandmother's son and his mother's brother, the alleged purpose being to maximize the mother's chances of remarrying. According to his grandmother, a prospective suitor would be much more likely to marry a childless woman than one with a son. In telling me all this, the patient made no comment about his own reaction to it. He gave no indication that having to play the role he did had caused him any special concern. It was just a stupid nuisance, apparently, that he had to be sure not to betray the fact that his mother was really his mother and not his sister whenever a strange man came calling.

By the time of his anxiety attack the patient was grown and self-supporting. His mother had died about a year before I first saw him, and his grandmother decided that, since he was grown up and self-supporting, it was time for him to have a place of his own. Hence the shopping expedition for household goods, an expedition on which he was accompanied by his grandmother, who picked out for him what he would need in his new home. It was in that setting that the patient had a severe anxiety attack.

Although the patient himself was unaware of any meaningful connection between his symptom and his family history, as he outlined it for me, modern conflict theory posits just such a connection, since he went from telling me the one to telling me the other. According to modern conflict theory, if one thought is followed by another, there must be a meaningful connection between the two, and in this case the later course of the analysis supplied the unconscious connection. The patient had grown up with the conviction, much as he tried to deny it to himself, that both his mother and his father would have preferred that he had never been born and that even his grandmother, despite her protestations of devotion, would have liked to be rid of him. Her insistence that he leave her and live alone intensified his conflict over the aggressive and sexual wishes associated with his conviction that he had been unwanted all his life to such a degree that he developed an anxiety attack in the store and was impelled to come for treatment. Indeed, looking back, I would venture the guess that he unconsciously looked for me to replace the grandmother he was being forced to leave. But that aside, isn't it clear that this patient's precipitating symptom was a potentially rich source of information that deserved (and, as it turned out, repaid) analysis?

I don't wish to give the impression that symptoms are necessarily quickly or easily analyzed. Quite the reverse is often the case. I wish only to emphasize that one should always view a symptom as something to be analyzed whenever possible. It may take weeks or months, sometimes even years, to discover what the conflicts are that underlie a symptom, but one should always be thinking about what they are, and one should be alert to analytic material that offers the possibility of answering the questions, "What conflicts are responsible for this symptom?" and "Why has it flared up anew (or disappeared, for that matter) just now?"

The example I have chosen was of a symptom that appeared before analysis began, but what I have just said applies equally to symptoms that appear or recur during analysis. They are just as potentially revealing as a dream or, for that matter, anything else a patient may say or do. Everything, according to modern conflict theory, can lead to a better understanding of a patient's conflicts and compromise formations if and when a patient is able to talk about it freely. Everything is grist for the analytic mill. And, as my example also illustrates, thoughts that follow one another are meaningfully related to one another.

Attention to Avoidance in Analysis

The knowledge that everything is potentially grist for the analytic mill guides one also in the following way. If a patient consistently avoids either the subject of sex or aggression, or both, it's incumbent on the analyst, sooner or later, to call the fact to the patient's attention and to suggest that the patient think and talk about the fact that this is so. Failure to talk about either subject or, for that matter, about any topic which the analyst believes to be significant for the patient, is an important communication. What it communicates is that the patient is using avoidance and/or denial as a way of defending against some sexual and/or aggressive wish(es) of childhood origin. As is the case with any important communication, the patient's thoughts (= associations) about avoiding one or another subject are potentially useful.

Inexact Interpretations

Ever since Strachey (1934) published his paper on inexact interpretation that topic bobs up from time to time. When it does, especially in supervision, I make the same response. There's no such thing as a perfect, exact, and complete interpretation. Every interpretation, however apt, is at best only a partial one. If an interpretation is at least somewhere near the mark, it is likely to be useful in furthering the work of analysis. In other words, if an interpretation is not way off the mark, it's fine. True, one should always try to be as close to the mark as possible. Second thoughts about how one could have said it better or at a better time are to be encouraged. Such self-criticism improves one's skills in a way that's always desirable. But the real test of an interpretation is whether it furthers the analytic work. If it does, one should not regret having made it.

A Line of Interpretation

Any conjecture that deals with an important aspect of a patient's conflicts should be expected to give rise to interpretations that will require many repetitions. One cannot expect substantial change in a patient's compromise formation(s) to result from presenting one's conjecture a single time, no matter how valid and substantial the conjecture is. The interpretive work of analysis is a matter of following lines of interpretation, not of interpreting something and then paying no further attention to it. An example may help clarify what I mean.

The patient was a young woman with a great flair for dramatic narrative. It was always a pleasure to listen to what she had to say about what was going on in her life. After a while, however, it became apparent that she rarely talked about the serious, ongoing problems that had brought her to analysis. The interpretation offered was that her interesting recitals served the purpose of diverting attention from the compromise formations that troubled her. She was obviously impressed by this and realized that she had indeed been focusing on trivia in order to avoid thinking about her very real problems. For a short time thereafter she spoke about them in a much more sober fashion. But the one correct interpretation didn't end the matter. It was necessary to make the same interpretation, though of course not always in just the same words, over and over again as her analysis proceeded. What was needed, as is always the case, was a line of interpretation, not a single intervention.

Conflict, Compromise Formation, and the Conduct of Analysis

As I said earlier, an analyst should always be wondering, "Why?" And modern conflict theory guides one in trying to answer that question. An analyst, like myself, who is convinced of its validity is persuaded that what he or she is listening to gives some clue as to the nature of and the interaction between certain childhood sexual and aggressive wishes, the calamities associated with them that give rise to anxiety and depressive affect, and the defenses whose function is to minimize the unpleasurable affects. Such an analyst listens, that is, with "a general notion of what to expect" (Freud 1924, p. 41). The answers to the "Why?" may be impossible to determine, but they are always there. Guided by a valid theory of how the mind develops, of the origin of childhood conflict and compromise formation, and of their role in later mental functioning, one expects to discover, gradually, more and more about the nature and origins of the conflicts and compromise formations of each individual patient. This is partly because of the analyst's increasing familiarity with the patient's history and habitual ways of reacting in various situations. In part as well, it is because the patient is increasingly able to express derivatives of childhood conflicts and compromise formations with less disguise and distortion (Brenner 1976). To the extent that analysis is successful, patients change during the course of analysis. Their compromise formations become more normal. They can get more pleasure from satisfying their pleasure-seeking wishes, with less unpleasure, and less need to defend against them and to punish themselves for gratifying them in fact and/or fantasy. As patients change in this way, both analyst and patient become able, usually bit by bit, to understand more clearly and fully what the patient's underlying conflicts are and the manner and extent to which they influence the patient's thought and behavior.

CHAPTER 5

The recognition that childhood conflict over sexual and aggressive wishes, however disguised, plays so great a role in all mental functioning throughout everyone's life is, I believe, the most important development in psychoanalysis in the past seventy-five years. Seventy-five or eighty years ago Freud (1923, 1926) revised his theory of mental functioning in two highly significant ways (Arlow and Brenner 1964). For one thing he said that repression is not the only defense, something that he had previously argued is the case. Till that time he had maintained that what distinguishes the normal from the pathological in mental life is whether or not it is accessible to consciousness. If it is, it's normal (= preconscious); if it's not, it is pathological (= part of the system Ucs.). The other change had to do with his theory of anxiety. Instead of his previous assertion that the anxiety that characterizes neuroses is due to a return of the repressed (= failure of repression), he reached the conclusion that conflict and defense begin in childhood.[1]

These changes in the psychoanalytic theory of mental development and functioning had major consequences for both the theory and the practice of psychoanalysis. Their consequence for psychoanalytic practice was the introduction of defense analysis. How to deal with a patient's defenses, subsumed till then under the heading of repression, had long been recognized as a problem of major importance and concern. But it was not till after the publication of the two monographs just referred to that analysts realized that a patient's defenses deserve to be *analyzed* rather than dealt with in some other way. The principal consequence of these changes for psychoanalytic theory was what is usually called *ego*

---

[1] See appendix 1.

psychology (Arlow and Brenner 1964). Together they constitute a watershed in the history of psychoanalysis.

The more recent realization that conflict is ubiquitous—that it is as important in and characteristic of what is properly called *normal* mental functioning as it is of what is called *pathological* mental functioning—is, I believe, a similar watershed, for the following reason. Currently, psychoanalysts, following Freud, conceive of the mind as a collection of agencies or structures. In the most widely current version, the structures are called *id, ego,* and *superego.* I have written at length elsewhere about why I consider such theories invalid.[2] The fact that a person's mind always functions in such a way as to achieve the maximum pleasurable gratification of sexual and aggressive wishes with a minimum of unpleasure means that there is no particular *part* of the mind that ignores the environment and that seeks only to gratify those wishes, while another *part* is attuned to the environment and therefore reacts to them with unpleasure. The whole mind reacts in each of those two ways, not just one part of it. As a result, *every* thought and action is a compromise formation (= modern conflict theory). *Every* thought and action is, at one and the same time, a gratification of pleasure-seeking wishes of childhood origin and a defense against those wishes—i.e., a way of minimizing the unpleasure associated with them.

It is interesting to see what consequences the adoption of modern conflict theory has for the understanding of how the mind works and for efforts to help minds work better, i.e., for psychoanalytic theory and for psychoanalytic practice. As a practicing psychoanalyst, I have been more concerned with the latter. My main concern has always been how to conduct therapy. My main interest has always been in practice. Any theory of the mind that is without effect on practice has never been of much interest to me. Whatever I have written about psychoanalysis has always been primarily addressed to those who are practicing psychoanalysts.

[2] See appendix 5.

My interest in therapy—in the psychoanalytic situation and the psychoanalytic method—is still as strong as ever. Though I no longer see patients, I am still actively engaged in teaching psychoanalytic technique and psychoanalytic theory as it relates to psychoanalytic technique, both to individual colleagues and to colleagues in groups. Still, I confess that something has changed in the last several years. The new perspective on how the mind works that is afforded by modern conflict theory fascinates me. It is a perspective that includes psychoanalytic technique, but much more besides. In this chapter, I hope to communicate to the reader something of the broader view of the human mind and its workings that I have found so illuminating.

Stages in Mental Functioning

The following is an example of what I mean. To my mind, modern conflict theory offers a panoramic view of mental development from the very beginning of life to its very end. It is a view that seems naturally divisible into a series of stages, not unlike the memorable account of the ages of man in Shakespeare's *As You Like It*.

The first three or so years of mental life are a period of progressive development. In that time, the brain, the organ of the mind, grows and changes in its functional capacity from month to month. There is no reason to doubt that, during that time, the mind functions in such a way as to achieve as much satisfaction of its wishes as it can and to avoid as much as possible in the way of unpleasure, just as it does subsequently throughout life. Nor is there reason to doubt that some events must inevitably occur during the first three years of every child's life that affect the functioning and development of the mind, either adversely or for the better. But at about the age of three, there is a major change. As described in chapter 2, the child's sexual and aggressive wishes for pleasurable satisfaction become progressively more extensive and explicit, and so do the fears and miseries that, in every child's mind, are associated with those wishes. Conflict and compromise formation make their appearance to an increasingly significant degree. They gradually become the rule in mental functioning and remain so throughout the rest of life. To be able to think more as adults do makes inevitable the beginning of a new phase of mental life.

As the years go by, children develop defenses against the sexual and aggressive wishes that have become associated with anxiety and depressive affect. They gradually enter a new stage, which Freud called *latency*. Compromise formations develop that deceive the children themselves and that are intended to deceive those about them into denying or ignoring the unwanted wishes for pleasurable satisfaction.

The next major change occurs at puberty, a time of life that has long been recognized as problematic in everyone's mental development. Until that time a part of every compromise formation is the reassuring awareness that one is, in fact, only a child, and as such unable to consummate the sexual and aggressive wishes that have given rise to such conflict and compromise formations. This awareness has, in most cases, a powerful defensive value. The realization, when one reaches puberty, that one is no longer a child, that one is big, strong, and sexually mature, negates that defense. New defenses are necessary, leading to new compromise formations, not infrequently to pathological ones. The psychological effect of entering puberty is always substantial and, in many cases, so great as to lead to turmoil, to mental illness, or, in the most extreme cases, even to death. To have a brain that can think and use language in adult fashion is one watershed in mental development. To have an adult endocrine and neuromuscular apparatus is another.

A fourth stage of mental functioning results from the changes of further aging. These are usually more dramatic in women (menopause) than in men, but by no means always so. In both sexes, the psychological effect of the climacteric is substantial enough to warrant speaking of a new stage of mental functioning.

These then are the stages in mental functioning that are indicated by modern conflict theory. First, a period from zero to three years; then one from ages three to six; another from six to twelve or so; another from twelve to nineteen or twenty; another from twenty to climacteric; and a final one postclimacteric. Modern conflict theory makes understandable and predictable the shifts from one period to the next and the reasons for them in a way and to a degree that I believe no other currently available theory of mental functioning and development can do. It gives one a bird's-eye view of mental life from the cradle to the grave.

Codes of Morality

But modern conflict theory doesn't cast light only on the vicissitudes of individual development; it illuminates broader perspectives as well. As I have indicated, it informs one that every phenomenon of adult mental life, even such diverse ones as jokes, hobbies, sexuality, and myths, have in common their origins in the compromise formations resulting from conflicts arising from the sexual and aggressive wishes of early childhood.

For example, it provides an explanation of the incest taboo. In our society, incest is not merely frowned upon; it is a crime. Yet it is also a favorite subject of literature and jokes. This seeming paradox is easily explained by modern conflict theory. The pleasurable sexual wishes of early childhood are focused on mother, father, brothers, and sisters. For reasons discussed in chapter 3, so are the associated fears and miseries. Children learn, beginning with the fateful years between three and six and progressively through the period from six to twelve, to disguise, distort, repress, and otherwise disavow their incestuous wishes. They defend against them. The wishes persist throughout life, but so do the defenses against them. Incest retains its fascination, but the desire to disavow that fascination retains its power as well.

In fact, the entire moral code that governs each individual's conduct is best understood in terms of compromise formation. Every such code is the result of an interaction among the sexual and aggressive wishes of early childhood, the anxiety and depressive affect connected with them, and defense. That aspect of the many compromise formations having to do with morality that arise from conflict resulting from childhood wishes, both sexual and aggressive, have as part of their ideational content being "good" or "bad" in the sense of conforming to or transgressing parental prescriptions for thought and behavior as experienced and fantasied in early childhood. They include feeling virtuous or the reverse, feeling remorseful, penitential, or self-punitive, and they have to do with atonement, forgiveness, reconciliation, and love.

For young children, morality means, essentially, feeling, thinking, and behaving in such a way as to avoid the familiar calamities of childhood: object loss, loss of love, and castration. The crucial questions in every child's mind are "What will win or forfeit parental approval and love?" and "What will rouse or dissipate parental wrath and retaliation?" These two questions provide the touchstone that decides whether something is good or bad in the sense of being moral or immoral, and they remain so, however consciously or unconsciously, throughout life.

The compromise formations that make up a person's moral code involve many sorts of defensive maneuvers. The most familiar, since it is the one that Freud (1923, 1933) emphasized, is identification with real and fantasied parental demands and prohibitions, as a result of which the child becomes strict, disciplinary, and punitive with itself. It is, however, by no means the only defensive maneuver that is involved in those compromise formations that make up each person's moral code. Another common one is an intensification of loving wishes toward the child's rival or rivals —a kind of reaction formation. Another is inhibition or repudiation of competitive wishes. Another, the substitution of oral or anal wishes for genital ones, is a variety of displacement. Another, the adoption of attitudes and behavior characterized by submissiveness. Even being sexually seductive to one's rival may have a defensive function in addition to the obvious pleasure-seeking one. The fact is that any thought and/or behavior that, in reality or in fantasy, furthers parental approval and avoids or undoes disapproval and punishment forms part of that individual's moral code (Brenner 1982, chapter 8).

An example of how widespread and important this phenomenon is came to my attention recently while watching television. A well-known and very popular author was being interviewed. In the course of the interview, he remarked that, once he has created a character in a work of fiction, he doesn't plan what that character will say and do. The character has "a life of its own" and says and does what it must and wishes to do. As anyone who is interested in the subject knows, this is a view that is frequently expressed by writers of fiction. It is obviously contrary to fact, as every author knows and would readily admit. The words and actions that an author attributes to a character that the author has dreamed up must come from the author's mind. The only other possible explanation is a magical one that relies on the idea of inspiration by a "higher" power or some similar, unscientific explanation. Why then should authors so often attribute to fictional characters lives of their own? Why should authors so often disown responsibility for their characters' words and actions, even when those words and actions are perfectly acceptable, even highly admired, by current adult standards? Why shouldn't they instead claim responsibility—even be proud of it? Why behave as though their accepted and admired fantasies have made them guilty?

This paradox is also readily explained by modern conflict theory. It is the provenance of such adult fantasies that accounts for what is so frequently observable in many authors' behavior. Like every other aspect of adult mental functioning, the fantasies that give rise to works of fiction are determinatively influenced by the compromise formations of each author's early childhood. Fear of retaliation and/or punishment for the "bad" wishes the author has expressed, plus the defensive thoughts and behavior to which such fears have given rise, are necessarily part of every work of fiction, as they are of every other aspect of mental functioning in adult mental life. In addition, the mere fact of having produced a successful or admired work of fiction may gratify sexual and aggressive wishes that must be defended against. No wonder authors so often talk of their characters as having independent lives of their own.

Creativity

The whole subject of creativity, of which being an author is a part, is worth discussing at this point. It is a subject on which modern conflict theory sheds much light.

In his famous dictionary, Johnson defined the word *create* as to form out of nothing, to cause to exist. His spiritual descendants, the lexicographers who put together the latest edition of Webster's dictionary, likewise defined *create* as "to bring into existence." Insofar as popular works of literature and dictionary definitions accurately reflect accepted usage one may say that the words *create* and, by extension, *creativity* are loaded words. They impute truly magic powers to those who do the creating, the power of making something out of nothing, the power of bringing into existence, as God is supposed to have done, according to the opening of the book of Genesis.

In addition, the adjective *creative* implies a significant value judgment. It is complimentary. Shakespeare was creative. So were Newton and Einstein, da Vinci and Michelangelo. One would not ordinarily call Genghis Khan, Hitler, or Stalin creative, even though each was instrumental in bringing into existence an organization that profoundly affected the lives of millions. To call someone creative is to imply admiration and approval, not the reverse.

Few people and even fewer scientists today believe that something material can be created out of nothing. What does seem to appear from nowhere, what does seem to be literally brought into existence, are thoughts and ideas. They and the objects to which they give rise—literature, art, scientific theories—are what deserve the adjective *creative*.

Freud's first approach to the problem of creativity was his monograph on Jensen's *Gradiva* (1907). In it he wrote that a writer of fiction

. . . directs his attention to the unconscious in his own mind, he listens to its possible developments and lends them artistic expression instead of suppressing them by conscious criticism. Thus he experiences from himself what we (psychoanalysts) learn from others—the laws which the activities of (the) unconscious must obey. [p. 92]

In a later article on Leonardo da Vinci, Freud's (1910) conclusion is quite evident that unconscious, repressed wishes can influence normal thought and behavior, but, and the *but* is a big one, only or primarily in creative individuals, in artists and especially in great artists. In fact, the belief still persists that the greater the artist, the freer that artist's access to the normally hidden sexual and aggressive wishes of childhood and to the conflicts associated with them. When such wishes influence the thought and behavior of ordinary folk, as in the slips and errors of daily life, Freud (1901) considered them pathological—the psychopathology of everyday life.

The idea that creative artists have special access to wishes and conflicts of childhood origin that are inaccessible to uncreative individuals unless those uncreative ones are neurotic (return of the repressed from repression) poses a serious problem. One way to solve the problem is to postulate that one must be more or less neurotic, or even psychotic, in order to be creative. Since everyone, creative or not, has plenty of evidence of neurotic difficulties, it is not hard to adduce evidence that seems to support this thesis. One need only demonstrate evidence of neurotic compromise formation in creative individuals, which is not difficult to do. Unfortunately, however, one must at the same time assume that ordinary persons who are not creative have little or nothing in the way of neurosis troubling them, which is far from the truth.

Another solution to the problem is to equate creativity with neurosis and/or psychosis. Being creative is then viewed as the equivalent in an artist of a pathological compromise formation (= neurosis) in someone who has neither talent nor capacity for artistic creativity. The creative act is thus viewed as an alternative to succumbing to mental illness, an idea that artists themselves not infrequently put forward.

Kris (1952) suggested still another possible solution, which he called *regression in the service of the ego*. His idea was that creative activity takes place in an altered ego state, one in which the creative individual has temporarily regressed to a more infantile, less mature mode of mental functioning. The analogy would be to the sort of regression that Freud (1900) attributed to mental functioning during dreaming. Just as a dreamer has access to the wishes and conflicts of childhood that are normally inaccessible during waking life, so a creative individual, Kris suggested, has equal or similar access to those wishes and conflicts during an act of creation.

I suggest that a better explanation than any of the ones just summarized is offered by a recognition of the fact that conflict and compromise formation are ubiquitous in mental life (Brenner 1982). The part played in creativity by the conflicts originating in childhood sexual and aggressive wishes is no different from the part they play in every other aspect of mental life. Creativity is no different from everyday mental functioning with respect to its dynamics; what is special about creativity has to do not with its psychodynamics. To put the matter more positively, everyone is creative all the time, every day. Every thought, plan, and action is a creative compromise formation, dynamically speaking, however mundane and ordinary it may be. Everyone produces a constant stream of compromise formations, whether awake or asleep, each of which is a unique creation without being in the least creative in the colloquially accepted meaning of the word.

Creativity is not a word to be used lightly in its colloquial meaning. It is an accolade. It is not to be bestowed on universal, everyday mental activity. Implicit in the colloquial concept of creativity is a value judgment, one adopted from the culture of society. What it signifies in our society is not just novelty of thought or action, or even thought and action that are unique as well as novel. It signifies, in addition, that the mental functioning of the person called *creative* is judged by the members of the society in which she or he lives to be *successfully* innovative. It signifies that the compromise formation(s) called *creative* are admirable and useful ones, ones that other members of society wish they could do, too.

To underline the point that the current, shared opinion about creativity is culturally based, it may be recalled that not all societies at all times thought highly of innovations, successful or not. There was a time in Western European history when the ideal was to conform, to do one's duty to God and master, and to shun change and innovation. When Galileo proposed his innovative idea about the solar system, an idea that is today considered to be highly creative, his masters in the church judged him to be heretical, not creative, and would have put him to death had he not recanted. The same sort of variability in judgment is apparent in the field of art. At the time when Van Gogh was unknown and disregarded as an artist, a painter named Bouguereau was widely acclaimed as a creative genius. Fifty years later, none but a very few had ever heard of Bouguereau, while Van Gogh was a name on everyone's lips. What is deemed creative today may be looked on as banal tomorrow. What is unnoticed or despised today may inspire universal admiration and praise after the death of its creator. There is a joke long current in musical circles to the effect that the definition of a musical genius is a dead composer.

In brief, creativity, like beauty, lies in the eyes and mind of the beholder, not in the psychodynamics of the individual who is called *creative*, however justified the appellation may be. It is the value judgment of one's fellow creatures that decides whether one is to be called creative or not. If one leaves that judgment to one side, everyone deserves to be called creative at every moment. As far as mental life is concerned, both men and women are creative by nature. Those who are honored by being *called* creative are the special few whose creative products are admired and prized, the special few whose creations are judged to be successfully innovative by members of the society to which they belong. The dynamics of the creative process are just as present in the creation of a piece of pulp fiction as in the creation of *Anna Karenina* or *War and Peace*. What distinguishes products that are rated as trash from those that are considered to be "truly creative" are their formal characteristics, not their dynamics. And the formal characteristics are, in large part at least, determined by societal norms. If there are any formal criteria of creativity, as we use the term, or, for that matter, of beauty, that are absolute in the sense of being independent of societal norms, they have yet to be convincingly demonstrated.

Daydreams

No knowledge of psychoanalysis is necessary to realize that daydreams have to do with unfulfilled wishes. Everyone knows from experience as well as by information from others that one often imagines in a daydream or reverie that what one wishes for is actually in one's grasp. Lovers parted from one another imagine they are blissfully together. Children daydream of being grown up. In fantasy they are attractive, accomplished, and successful at whatever they do. A hungry person daydreams of eating a delicious meal; a thirsty one, of drinking; a tired one, of rest. True, there are exceptions. There are unpleasant, even frightening daydreams. In the great majority of daydreams, however, conscious wishes are consciously gratified.

All that I have said so far is common knowledge. What psychoanalytic data have to add is this. Daydreams, at least in adult life, are never simply fantasies that gratify conscious wishes or needs. They are compromise formations that derive from conflicts arising from childhood wishes even when, at the same time, they are determinatively influenced by conscious wishes. The following will serve to illustrate the role of each factor.

A 28-year-old male patient was annoyed with me for having to change his daily schedule to suit my convenience. He felt like telling me to go to hell. At the same time, he was ashamed of himself for being angry, since he was appreciative of the help he felt he was getting and was generally well disposed toward me. Under these circumstances, he had the following daydream, which he reported at the start of an analytic session.

As he was walking toward my office on his way to the session, he imagined turning the corner and seeing police cars and an ambulance in front of the office entrance. There had been a terrible accident, he imagined. A patient had become violent and had shot me. I was lying on the floor in a pool of blood. When he got to that point, the patient revised his fantasy. I was not shot. An insane patient was threatening me with a gun, but the patient was there. He grappled with my assailant and disarmed him before he could shoot me.

The patient's associations began with a motion picture that he had seen the evening before, which was filled with scenes of violence and murder. It had also contained frankly erotic scenes that had been sexually stimulating to the patient. In one scene, a man seduced the widow of someone he himself had murdered. This had horrified the patient and yet, at the same time, he had been fascinated by the idea of someone doing such a thing. Later he mentioned that one of the characters, an older man, had reminded him of his father—not that he really looked like him; it was just that the glasses he wore were like the ones his father used to wear. The patient then went on to speak of how reliable his father had always been, how he could always count on him, and from there to his annoyance at me for the change in schedule.

In this daydream, the patient's conscious feelings for me were expressed in a form clearly influenced by the film he had seen the night before. He gratified his anger by imagining that someone had killed me or, in the revised version, had threatened to do so. He gratified his friendly feelings by rescuing me. The guilt he consciously felt for wishing to tell me to go to hell, as well as the need to ward off his anger, found expression in the fantasy that it was not he but another patient who was my murderer, and in the fact that, in fantasy, he exposed himself to danger by grappling with my assailant.

These motives were all conscious. The patient was readily aware of them. However, they were no means the only determinants of the patient's daydream, nor even, in this instance, the ones that were of principal importance. The patient's father had been shot to death in his office by an employee who was mentally ill, when the patient was in early adolescence. He had missed his father very much afterward and had often imagined scenes in which he had been in his father's office, had disarmed the assailant, and had saved his father's life. The patient expressed in his daydream not only his consciously ambivalent wishes and feelings for me, but also murderous and loving wishes and feelings for his father, which had been transferred to me as his analyst. Moreover, the transferred wishes and feelings had not by any means originated during his adolescence, though they had been powerfully influenced by his father's murder at that time. As his associations suggested, his transferred wishes and feelings were of childhood origin. An important stimulus for the daydream had been provided by the sexually exciting scenes of the film he had seen the night before, in which a man was portrayed as murdering another man and seducing his widow, something the patient had found to be both horrifying and fascinating, and to which he associated thoughts of his own father.

Thus, without presuming to say that the daydream under discussion has been fully or exhaustively analyzed, one can say on the basis of the evidence available that it was a compromise formation in which the components of a conflict of childhood origin were blended. In it were combined oedipal wishes, castration anxiety—symbolized by my being shot and by the patient's disarming my assailant—and defense.

For my present purpose, a more thorough, more nearly complete analysis of the daydream is unnecessary, since it would do no more than reinforce the statement that this patient's daydream was a compromise formation that resulted from psychic conflict originating in childhood.

The conscious wishes of everyday life vary with everyday circumstance, with daily needs, impressions, and interests. The wishes and conflicts of childhood, however, persist essentially unchanged throughout one's life, even though largely unconsciously. The result is that, while one's daydreams constantly vary in accordance with one's conscious wishes, they also, in a very important sense, remain the same, since they reflect the various components of conflicts associated with and originated by sexual and aggressive wishes of childhood origin. Thus, for example, the patient just referred to had repeated daydreams of saving his father's life during his adolescence. His boyhood reveries were regularly concerned with parricide in the same way as was the transference daydream just discussed.

Another patient, during childhood, had recurrent fantasies of being in the army and operating a machine gun. In his daydreams, he killed thousands of imaginary enemies. He also had a buddy, a beloved comrade, in each daydream. The buddy would always be wounded, nearly fatally, only to be saved by the patient in a heroic, self-sacrificing way.

In this case, the military setting was determined by external circumstances, namely, the Second World War. The patient, a boy during the war, consciously wished to be grown up and a manly soldier, but the unconscious determinants of his repeated daydream were both more complex and more important.

The patient's playmate in real life, his real buddy, was a sister, four years younger than himself, who was his mother's darling. The patient's jealous rage encompassed the entire family, but it could never be expressed openly. Instead, it found a partial or substitute outlet in fantasies of patriotic slaughter. His jealous wish to take his sister's place as the beloved girl baby of his family was associated with intense castration anxiety, which also found expression in his daydreams, as did defense. In his daydreams, it was not he who had become a girl, but his sister who had become a man. Moreover, he had a large machine gun in his hands as symbolic reassurance that his penis was intact. In addition, he did not kill his sister in fantasy. It was the bad enemy who tried to kill her, while he rescued her and tended her wounds with loving care, always at the risk of his own life.

Thus daydreams are normal psychic phenomena that are compromise formations resulting from psychic conflicts of childhood origin. This is important in itself, but it also has broader implications for many other aspects of psychic functioning. Most daydreams are of purely personal significance to the daydreamer. They are disclosed to another person only under special circumstances, one of which is being a patient in psychoanalysis. There are daydreams, however, that are communicated to others and come to play an important role in the psychic lives of those to whom they have been told. Daydreams are the basis of folk tales, of fictional literature, of myths, and of religious beliefs. They can become communal by being adopted by persons other than the person who originated them (Sachs 1942).

Religion, Atheism, and Politics

No aspect of societal life is more interesting psychologically than religion. Since the dawn of history, it has occupied a central position in the great drama called civilization, but it is only in the last two centuries that there has been even a threat to its preeminently important role.

A cosmogony, a moral and ethical code, and a catalogue or system of rewards for obeying the code and of punishments for transgressing it—these are constituents of every known religion (Freud 1933). Every religion tells its believers how they and the earth on which they live came to be, as well as how to behave so as to prosper and be happy. Not every religion has an anthropomorphic god, as do the Judeo-Christian-Moslem ones. Some have many gods in human form, some have animal or other gods, some have no gods whatsoever. Some promise life after death, while others do not. Some are warlike, while others preach peace and brotherhood. Whatever their differences may be in these and other respects, all religions teach, prescribe, and protect or threaten in the ways Freud described. Religions treat adults as parents treat children (Freud 1933).

If Freud's assessment is correct, as I believe it is, religion is the outgrowth into adult life of a child's relation to its parents. Since, from a child's side, this relation is so largely composed of sexual and aggressive wishes and of the conflicts to which those wishes give rise, it comes as no surprise that religious beliefs and practices are compromise formations.

Though it is impossible to make a really reliable estimate, it is probably correct to say that religious beliefs play an important role in the conscious mental lives of most people on the earth today. At the same time, it is clear that a growing percentage of the world's population does not subscribe to any religious belief, and that religion as a social institution is on the decline.

The most important factor in this decline is almost surely the psychological impact of the scientific and technological developments of the past three centuries. Galileo is chiefly responsible for having initiated the events that are leading to just the consequences the Roman Curia hoped to prevent by forcing him to recant and then holding him prisoner for the rest of his life. It took many decades, however, and the discoveries of many scientists who followed Galileo, before the progress of science, great as it was, affected the religious beliefs of mankind to a noticeable degree. As recently as the time of the First World War, every government espoused some religious belief. Not a single one was officially atheistic. By now, the situation is substantially different. The governments of two countries, China and, as of 1982, the Soviet Union, whose combined populations at that time included one-third of the population of the globe, have condemned all religions. So have the governments of many smaller countries. What has happened to the religious beliefs of these one and a half billion people?

No doubt millions still cling to conscious belief in one religion or another, but millions of others are consciously in agreement with the doctrine that all religions are factually incorrect. They are convinced that the gods their parents or grandparents worshipped are nonexistent; that assurances of a life after death are illusory, whether those assurances are promises of heaven or threats of hell; and that religious cosmologies are nothing but the charming myths of ignorant, unscientific people, however poetically gifted they may have been.

Since religion comes from sources in psychic life that are as deep as psychoanalysis has shown them to be, since religious beliefs have been such useful compromise formations for countless generations of mankind, it seems impossible that religion could simply disappear without a substitute. There is, by now, more than enough evidence to show that Marxist socialism neither alters childhood wishes nor eliminates the conflicts associated with them. The psychic forces that have motivated people to participate in organized religion for millennia are as strong among inhabitants of socialist countries as they are in those of the rest of the world. What, then, are their manifestations in an atheistic, irreligious society?

To answer this question reliably, one would have to have psychoanalytic data on which to base one's answer. One would have to assess the accumulated relevant findings of the analyses of many consciously atheistic persons, preferably of the second or third generation, who live in officially atheistic countries. Unfortunately, there are no such findings available for study. The officially atheistic countries of the world today, like many others that officially subscribe to one or another religious belief, are police states in which all mental health workers are dependent on the state for their livelihood. Under such conditions, it is virtually impossible either to learn to do psychoanalysis or to practice it if one has been trained elsewhere.

One might hope to substitute data obtained from the analyses of atheistic patients living in societies that are not officially atheistic, but in which large segments of the populace are, in fact, atheists. The answer suggested by such data from this source as are available is that religious beliefs tend to persist, though disavowed. Often enough the same thing, or something similar, is true for religious practices as for religious beliefs. For example, atheistic patients in modern society react to religious holidays as do those who professedly believe in their significance: they dream of babies at Christmastime and of infanticide or parricide at the time of Passover and Easter. They call on God to bless themselves and to curse others. They enjoy sacred music—a Bach cantata or a mass by Mozart, for instance—while professing disinterest in the words for which the music was written. Not infrequently they attend religious services that, at the same time, they sincerely maintain have no meaning for them whatsoever. In short, they seem to have adopted at least some of the religious beliefs and practices of the society in which they were born and raised, while consciously disavowing both belief and practice. In attempting to assess the significance of such data, it must be kept in mind that they come in large part, if not entirely, from the analyses of persons who were exposed to some kind of religious influence during childhood, or even to formal religious instruction.

The rather unsatisfactory data available to bear on the question point in the direction that religious beliefs and practices persist in the minds of atheists, though disavowed, repressed, or defended against in other ways. For how many generations they would continue to persist in an avowedly atheistic society, there is no way of knowing. Perhaps the following, admittedly speculative answer to the question posed originally has some merit.

It may be that politics and political beliefs occupy the same psychological position and serve the same psychological functions in the officially atheistic countries of the world today as religion and religious beliefs do elsewhere. In atheistic countries, there are political processions and festivals for people to participate in, instead of religious ones. Instead of religious icons, there are political banners and pictures. Instead of divine or semidivine personages of the past, there are Marx, Engels, and Lenin. Instead of priests, there are political leaders who command obedience, love, and reverential awe.

In addition, there is a strong moral trend in socialist and communist teachings as they exist today. Belief and conformity are not merely rewarded in a material sense; they are valued as good. Believers in socialism who support the regime are considered to be good in a moral sense. Unbelievers and those who are antagonistic to the regime are judged as bad by the community at large. In addition, socialism promises reward for good behavior and punishment for bad, just as religions do. It promises that the advent of true socialism will bring with it a kind of heaven on earth, the equivalent of the stereotyped folk tale ending, "and they lived happily ever after."

What has just been said about the psychology of politics in countries with atheistic regimes in the world today is not intended to discredit in any way either the economic and political theories of socialism or its ideal goal of economic plenty for all. Indeed, if it is true that imitation is the sincerest form of flattery, all the major capitalist countries of the world have only the highest praise for the socialist ideal of social justice. Without exception, they offer to their citizens the same promise of material prosperity and security for all. My speculation goes only to the point that, in nonreligious societies, the psychic trends otherwise expressed in religious practices and beliefs have made a kind of religion of politics and politicians.

One should add that this development was neither intended nor foreseen. The reformers who were the architects and leaders of the revolutions that created the nonreligious societies of today had no conscious desire for those societies to become themselves a kind of religion. Quite the contrary. Such an idea would have been abhorrent to them. Nevertheless, this may be what has happened.

If so, it is not really a novelty in societal organization. In many societies, men and women have deified their rulers from the most ancient times. In Egypt and in the valley of the Tigris and the Euphrates rivers, where the first empires we know of arose, king, high priest, and god were one and the same. Even after the birth of rationalism in the golden age of Greece, Aristotle's pupil, Alexander, was deified, as were countless other Greek and Roman rulers who succeeded him. It seems strange to think of a living person who claims to be a god, and even stranger when such a person is considered to be one by others, yet until very recently, most of the world was ruled, at least in name, by men and women who claimed to have been selected for the position of king or queen by God himself. In their own opinion and in the opinion and belief of their subjects, they ruled by divine right—*Dei gratia*. Even today, the conservative faithful of the Roman Catholic Church consider the Pope (in Italian, *il Papa* = father), whose official title is simply bishop of Rome, to be the direct representative of God on earth. This position, psychologically speaking, surely is close to that of a living deity—not the equal of one of the great gods, to be sure, but like them, though on a lesser scale.

The fact is that analytic data strongly support the conclusion that anyone who is looked up to as older and as being in a position of superior wisdom can and often does unconsciously represent a parent. This generalization does not apply only to authoritarian regimes, whether they be religious or atheistic ones. Any ruling establishment is not just imposed from above. It is supported from below as well, and the attitude of the humble toward their rulers in any society is inevitably a reflection of childhood wishes and of the conflicts attendant on them. The president of a republic is unconsciously viewed as a father no less than is God, or a dictator, or a divinely anointed king, or an imperial demigod. The accepted sobriquet of the first president of the United States, George Washington, is "the father of his country." It is given to him as the first president. It was never given to Franklin, Jefferson, Madison, or Hamilton, all of whom arguably played indispensable roles in the unification of the thirteen colonies, something Washington also did. It is Washington, the successful warrior and the first president, who is by consensus revered as the country's father.

What differences there are in the attitude of the general public to a god, a demigod, a divinely appointed king, a dictator, and a president who was elected by the people themselves seem to be differences of degree. The differences seem to lie in the forcefulness with which a particular society or social organization insists that, *in reality*, one person, or a relatively few people, do indeed possess the attributes with which young children endow their parents: that they are so wise as to be omniscient, so strong as to be omnipotent, and so good as to be without sin or flaw. That to love and obey them is to be good, i.e., to be deserving of love and reward in return, while to fail to love and obey is to be bad and to deserve whatever punishment they impose.

The more closely any religious organization or political system approaches such criteria, the more obviously it is an adult reproduction of the psychic life of childhood, and the more obviously does it serve the function of a compromise formation for each of its members. With respect to both politics and religion, the urge to duplicate the world of childhood is unmistakable. It is observable in societies today no less than in those of fifty centuries ago.

It must be apparent that this discussion of religion and, to a less extent, of sociopolitical organization has merely touched on one aspect of two immensely complex subjects. I have done no more than to adduce evidence in favor of the view that the psychology of each is that of compromise formation arising from childhood wishes. Even in this task I have limited myself. I have said little of the role of sensual or libidinal wishes as compared with the role of aggressive ones, for example, although the importance of each is, if not equal, at least fully comparable. As an example, female members of many Christian religious orders marry God (Jesus) on entering that order.

I say this to ensure that it will not be wrongly assumed that I believe that what I have said represents anything approaching a thorough exposition of even the psychology of the aspects of human psychic life that I have been discussing, to say nothing of a thorough exposition of the whole of them. Whatever generalizations one may suggest at present about the psychology of religion or of sociopolitical organizations on the basis of a knowledge of psychoanalytic psychology cannot be more than provisional. However, when one considers how little is known in either field and how much remains to be learned, one may be persuaded, as I am, that even formulations that cannot yet be adequately substantiated or satisfactorily tested nonetheless deserve serious consideration, provided their provisional nature is kept in mind.

Power and Corruption

As a final generalization of this sort, the following is of interest.

The two hundred years since the French and American revolutions have often been called the age of revolution. Never before has revolution been so widespread. Never before have so many revolutions been so successful in their immediate aim of overthrowing existing governments and establishing new ones, each allegedly based on the by-now universally accepted principles of liberty, equality, fraternity, popular sovereignty, and the rights of man.

In the course of recording these many political upheavals, it has not escaped the attention of at least some historians that a foe of tyranny, once successful in deposing the ruling tyrant, often becomes equally tyrannical. The explanation most often cited to account for this sequence of events is the epigram attributed to the British historian Acton, to the effect that power corrupts, while absolute power corrupts absolutely.

Modern conflict theory suggests that being a revolutionary, like being a tyrant, a priest, a demigod, or anything else, for that matter, has important determinants that derive from conflicts arising from childhood sexual and aggressive wishes. It suggests that to be a revolutionary is to choose that particular compromise formation as a vocation. If this is indeed the case, as I believe it is, it is easy to surmise some of the psychological determinants likely to be responsible for the evolution of liberators into tyrants.

As noted earlier, the relation between adult subject and ruler, tyrant or not, reflects and, in important respects, repeats the relation between child and parent. It is a compromise formation that arises from conflicts over childhood wishes, among which are included wishes to supplant the parent and to assume his or her place in the family constellation. The data available from the psychoanalysis of patients suggest that admiration, envy, and a desire to imitate are among the determinants of the vocational choice and behavior of political revolutionaries. Whether they are aware of it or not, they wish to supplant and to imitate whomever they revolt against. It is to be expected that such a ruler would follow in the same mold. If the deposed ruler was a tyrant, one would expect the deposer to become one as well. If what one wishes is to become a tyrant, the power one has achieved enables one to become one.

Modern conflict theory suggests that power does not "corrupt." There have been, after all, beneficent despots as well as evil-doing ones. Modern conflict theory suggests that power, i.e., the power to coerce other persons to one's will, permits and even encourages the gratification of childhood wishes to do so—wishes that, in adult life, would otherwise find other means of gratification. As already noted, environmental circumstances simply set the stage for the drama of each person's life. Every individual, whether ruler or subject, master or slave, exploits whatever opportunities are at hand for gratification.

Conclusion

These are some of the ways by which modern conflict theory seems to me capable of expanding one's understanding of many aspects of the world in which we live. If my own experience is a reliable guide, the knowledge that *everything* in the way of thought and action is a compromise formation opens one's eyes to what appears indeed as a brave new world. What I have presented in this chapter is but a sample that I hope will stimulate others to go much farther than I have done.

EPILOGUE

To sum up as concisely as I can, when I use the word *psychoanalysis,* I mean by it modern conflict theory and the form of psychotherapy that is based upon it. Modern conflict theory is a set of propositions that conform to the credo or rules of natural science. Its subject matter is thoughts and feelings that have meaning and whose meanings are connected with one another sequentially in accordance with the idea of cause and effect. The organ of the mind is the brain, in particular, the forebrain. As the brain develops, so does the mind; psychoanalysis is a developmental psychology. When the brain becomes capable of acquiring language is when mental conflict begins.

Pleasure-seeking sexual and aggressive wishes, directed toward parents and siblings, inevitably become associated with unpleasurable affects (= anxiety and depressive affect). Since the mind functions both to achieve pleasure and to avoid unpleasure, mental conflict and compromise formation are the result. The pleasure-seeking sexual and aggressive wishes and the associated anxiety and depressive affects never disappear. They persist throughout life. What can and do change are the compromise formations to which the conflicts give rise. All the thoughts and feelings that make up our mental lives, both the ones called *normal* and the ones called *pathological,* are compromise formations resulting from conflicts over the sexual and aggressive wishes that first begin to be clearly recognizable in the fourth year.

Psychoanalysis as therapy is a form of psychotherapy that has as its aim the alteration of pathological compromise formations to normal ones. The patient reports his/her thoughts and feelings from moment to moment as fully as possible. From what the patient says (and does) plus what the analyst knows in addition about the patient's past and present life, the analyst forms conjectures about the patient's pathological compromise formations and communicates those conjectures to the patient with the expectation that, as the patient's insight into his/her conflicts and compromise formations grows, the desired changes in the patient's compromise formations will take place.

The observed data on which modern conflict theory is based include patients' speech and behavior in analytic settings, as well as a wide variety of observations of the thoughts and actions of children and adults in nonanalytic settings. Fantasies, both individually generated and adopted, and the actions associated with them, are among the data of observation that are of special value and importance in offering support for the conclusions about mental development and functioning that constitute modern conflict theory.

APPENDIX 1

I've chosen two examples to illustrate that Freud did not consider his conclusions (= theories) about mental functioning and development immune from correction and alteration. The first has to do with the changes he made in his concept of repression/defense; the second has to do with his theories of anxiety.

As soon as Freud gave up hypnotizing his patients and instead instructed them to say whatever came to their minds about the onset of their neurotic symptoms, it became evident to him that they struggled against (= resisted) remembering the memories he urged and commanded them to reproduce. It was on the basis of these observations that he concluded that the memories in question had not been simply forgotten, but had been consciously suppressed because of their painful and distressing nature, and he labeled the process *repression* in order to distinguish it from ordinary forgetting.

So Freud's earliest theory of repression was that certain individuals consciously suppress the memory of painful events and try to avoid remembering them. That theory was soon amended and expanded, however. Within a decade, as his clinical observations brought forth new data, he realized, to his surprise, that there is a basic pathogenic or predisposing factor for repression in adult life, namely, a sexual experience in childhood. And another important addition to the theory of repression was that it is not a process that is consciously initiated, but rather one that occurs unconsciously.

At first, then, Freud conceived of repression as something that is a precondition of pathology. It was only after he learned more about the psychology of dreams, of jokes, and of the slips and errors of daily life that he made another, far-reaching change in his theory of repression. He concluded that repression occurs in normal mental development as well as being a precursor of later psychopathology. His formulation was that, if there is too much repression of childhood sexual experiences and fantasies, the consequence in adult life is apt to be psychoneurosis; if there is too little, the consequence is one or more sexual perversions; if there is neither too much nor too little, the consequence is normal adult mental functioning.

So far, so good. Freud had progressively expanded his theory of repression and had even amended it by concluding that it is a process that is or can be an unconscious one, but none of this was what one can call a drastic revision of theory. At this point, however, Freud introduced some theoretical ideas concerning repression and anxiety that he was later to repudiate and/or alter in a major way. The sequence was as follows.

The sexual fantasies and experiences of childhood that become repressed are pleasurable during childhood, at least in the majority of cases. One of the factors responsible for their being repressed, Freud theorized, is that there are two kinds of repression. One is primal repression, the other, repression proper. One is a phenomenon of childhood, while the other occurs later in life. Primal repression is a consequence of the way the mind develops as children mature. Ethical and moral standards that are antithetic to some of the sexual fantasies and experiences of childhood are part of the system Pcs., and that system develops only after a child reaches the age of six years or so. Any sexual fantasies and memories from a still earlier time that are contrary to the ethical and moral standards of the developing Pcs. system have no access to that system. They remain in the system that was the only one at the earlier age, namely the system Ucs. But, said Freud, the system Pcs. as it develops, gains control of access to consciousness, of planned action, and of affective mental life. So the sexual fantasies and memories that are at odds with the child's developing Pcs. system come to lose access to consciousness and to motor and affective expression. This, Freud theorized, is primal repression. It isn't a result of conflict. It's a result of the timetable of mental development.

The other kind of repression, the kind that's associated with conflict and psychopathology, Freud proposed in his theory, is related to primal repression in this way. It may happen that primal repression fails, that is to say, that the memories and fantasies that are at odds with the standards of the Pcs. emerge or threaten to emerge from repression. Whenever that happens, anxiety arises and the Pcs. tries to re-repress the unwanted fantasies and memories. That sort of repression Freud conceived of as repression proper.

What I wish to make clear is that, in the theory of repression I have just outlined, Freud posited two kinds of repression. The first kind is determined by developmental chronology; the second, by anxiety and conflict.

Subsequently, Freud (1926) rescinded this theory and reverted to the theory that repression that characterizes that period of life for which he had coined the term, the latency period, is the result of conflict over childhood sexual fantasies and memories, rather than preceding such conflict. As illustrative examples of the data that prompted him to change his theory of repression, he chose two cases that he had previously presented in some detail. One was the case of "Little Hans" (Freud 1909), the other, the "Wolf Man" (Freud 1918). In fact, in 1926, he dropped the concept and the term *primal repression* altogether, and referred to repression in early life simply as the earliest and most "fundamental" kind of repression. One can see, therefore, that Freud was ready to alter or discard even very important parts of his theories of how the mind functions when he felt the data warranted it.

The same is true of his theories about anxiety. As late as 1926, his theory was that neurotic anxiety is to be distinguished from realistic anxiety. Realistic anxiety he identified as a normal reaction in any situation in which a real danger threatens. Neurotic anxiety, on the other hand, he attributed to the failure of (primal) repression, as outlined above. Until 1926, then, in fact his theory was that neurotic anxiety is altered libido—libido that has been altered by (primal) repression. He believed that when a previously repressed sexual wish escapes from repression (= return of the repressed), the affect that accompanies it is not the original one of sexual satisfaction or excitement. It is, instead, anxiety. The theory was that, just as badly stored wine will turn to vinegar, previously repressed libido can turn to anxiety.

In 1926, in *Inhibitions, Symptoms and Anxiety*, he abandoned this theory and substituted a different one that he believed fitted the observed facts better. The sexual wishes of early childhood, he said, arouse anxiety because children consider them dangerous. Children believe they may lead to any or all of various calamities: object loss, loss of love, castration, or retribution and/or punishment, and it is for that reason that they are repressed or otherwise defended against. Thus instead of contrasting neurotic anxiety to realistic anxiety, as he had previously done, he theorized that both are the reaction to the perception of danger—a major change in theory.

It should be added that he also believed that there is another form of anxiety that arises automatically whenever pleasure-seeking wishes are too intense to be satisfactorily mastered, as in very early childhood and, on occasion, in later life as well. When such an event occurs in adult life, Freud believed, the result is not a psychoneurosis, but what he called an "actual" neurosis. This part of Freud's theory of anxiety is not pertinent to the present discussion, however, since it underwent no substantial change in 1926. I have, in fact, included only enough of Freud's theories of repression and anxiety to make the point that he was ready to change any of his theories when he believed that new facts required it. Any who are interested to read more on either subject will find much fuller discussions of Freud's ideas on repression in Brenner 1957a, and of his ideas on anxiety in Brenner 1957b.

APPENDIX 2

The sense of the principle of psychic determinism is that, in the mind as in physical nature about us, nothing happens by chance or in a random way. Each psychic event is determined by the ones that preceded it. Events in our mental lives that may seem to be random and unrelated to what went on before are only apparently so. In fact, mental phenomena are no more capable of such a lack of causal connection with what preceded them than are physical ones. Discontinuity in this sense does not exist in mental life.

The understanding and application of this principle is essential for a proper orientation in the study of human psychology as well in its normal as in its pathological aspects. If we understand and apply it correctly, we shall never dismiss any psychic phenomenon as meaningless or accidental. We shall always ask ourselves, in relation to any such phenomenon in which we are interested, "What caused it? Why did it happen so?" We ask ourselves these questions because we are confident that an answer to them exists. Whether we can discover the answer quickly and easily is another matter, to be sure, but we know that the answer is there.

An example of this approach to psychic phenomena is the following. It is a common experience of everyday life to forget or mislay something. The usual view of such an occurrence is that it is "an accident," that it "just happened." Yet a thorough investigation of many such "accidents" during the past hundred years by psychoanalysts, beginning with the studies of Freud himself, has shown that they are by no means as accidental as popular judgment considers them to be. On the contrary, each such "accident" can be shown to have been caused by a wish or intent of the person involved, in strict conformity with the principle of mental functioning that we have been discussing.

To take another example from the realm of everyday life, Freud discovered, and the analysts who followed him have confirmed, that the common, yet remarkable and mysterious phenomena of sleep called dreams follow the same principle of psychic determinism. Each dream, indeed each image in each dream, is the consequence of other psychic events, and each stands in a coherent and meaningful relationship to the rest of the dreamer's life.

If we turn to the phenomena of psychopathology, we shall expect the same principle to apply, and indeed, psychoanalysts have repeatedly confirmed that expectation. Each neurotic symptom, whatever its nature, is caused by other mental processes, despite the fact that patients themselves often consider the symptom to be foreign to their whole being and quite unconnected with the rest of their mental lives. The connections are there, nonetheless, and are demonstrable despite the patient's unawareness of their presence.

At this point, we can no longer avoid recognizing that we are talking not only about the principle (= hypothesis) of psychic determinism, but also about the hypothesis that there are mental processes of whose existence and significance persons are themselves unaware or unconscious.

In fact, the relation between these two hypotheses is so intimate that one can hardly discuss the one without bringing in the other. It is precisely the fact that so much of what goes on in our minds is unconscious, that is, unknown to ourselves, that accounts for the *apparent* discontinuities in our mental lives. When a thought, a feeling, an accidental forgetting, a dream, or a pathological symptom seems to be unrelated to what went on in the mind beforehand, it is because its causal connection is with some *unconscious* mental process, rather than with a conscious one. If the unconscious cause or causes can be discovered, then all apparent discontinuities disappear and the causal change or sequence becomes clear.

A simple example of this would be the following. A person finds her- or himself humming a tune without having any idea of how it came to mind. This apparent discontinuity in the subject's mental life is resolved, in our particular example, by the testimony of a bystander, who tells us that the tune in question was *heard* by the subject a few moments before it entered conscious thought, apparently from nowhere. It was a sensory impression, in this case an auditory one, that caused the subject to hum the tune. Since the subject was unaware of hearing the tune, the subjective experience was of a discontinuity of thought, and it required the bystander's testimony to remove the appearance of discontinuity and to make clear the causal chain.

The example just given was chosen for its simplicity. In fact it is rare for an unconscious mental process—in this case an auditory perception—to be discovered so simply and easily. The natural question to ask is whether there is any more general method for discovering mental processes of which a person is unaware. Can they be observed directly? If not, how did Freud discover the frequency and importance of unconscious processes in everyone's mental life?

The most useful and reliable method we have at present for studying unconscious mental processes is the technique that Freud evolved over a period of several years. This technique he called *psychoanalysis* for the very reason that he was able, with its help, to discern and detect psychic processes that would otherwise have remained hidden and unsuspected. It was during the same years in which he was developing the method of psychoanalysis that Freud became aware, with the help of his new technique, of the importance of unconscious mental processes in the mental life of every individual, whether mentally sick or healthy.

The data are particularly full and clear when one uses the analytic technique that Freud devised. However, there are other sources of data that furnish evidence for the fundamental proposition that unconscious mental processes have the capacity to produce effects on both thought and action.

Evidence of this sort that is of the nature of an experiment is provided by the well-known facts of posthypnotic suggestion. A subject is hypnotized and, while in a trance, is told something that she/he is to do after she/he has been roused from the trance. For example, "When the clock strikes two, you will get up from your chair and open the window." While still in the trance, the subject is also instructed to have no recollection of what happened during the hypnotic session. Shortly after the subject is roused, the clock strikes two and the subject goes over and opens the window. If asked, "Why did you do that?" the answer may be "I felt warm" or "I just felt like it." The point is that the subject is not conscious when opening the window of the real reason for doing so. A truly unconscious mental process (obedience to a command) has had a dynamic or motivational effect on thought and behavior.

Other evidences of this fact may be derived from clinical, or even general observation. It is well known from many sources, for example, the journals and logs of early Arctic expeditions, that starving men often dream of food and of eating. It is easy to recognize that it is hunger that gives rise to such dreams, and of course the men are quite consciously aware of their hunger when they are awake, but *during their sleep,* when they are dreaming of gorging themselves at banquets, they are *not conscious* of hunger, but only of a dream of satiation, so that we can say that at the time the dream was dreamed, something was going on *unconsciously* in the dreamer's mind that gave rise to the dream images that were consciously experienced.

Other dreams of convenience, such as those in which dreamers dream they are drinking only to wake to the realization of being thirsty, or dreams of urination or defecation from which one wakes with an urge to relieve oneself, similarly demonstrate that, during sleep, the unconscious activity of the mind can produce a conscious result—in these cases, that an unconscious bodily sensation and the wishes connected with it can give rise to a conscious dream of the desired satisfaction or relief. Such a demonstration is important in itself and can be made without any special technique of observation. By means of the psychoanalytic technique, however, Freud was able to demonstrate that behind every dream, there are active unconscious thoughts and desires, and thus to establish as a *general rule* that when dreams occur, they are caused by mental activity that is unconscious to the dreamer and that would remain so without the use of the psychoanalytic technique.

There is another group of phenomena to which Freud called attention that also demonstrate how unconscious mental activities can affect conscious behavior. Like dreams, these are normal features of mental life; like dreams, also, they had been previously neglected because they could not be fruitfully studied until the psychoanalytic method had been evolved. They occur in waking life rather than in sleep and are what we call, in general, slips: slips of the tongue, of the pen, of memory, and similar, related actions for which there is no very exact, generic name in English. As in the case of dreams, some slips are clear and simple enough for us to be able to guess with a high degree of accuracy and conviction what their unconscious meaning is. It is notoriously easy to forget something that is unpleasant or annoying, like paying a bill, for example. The amorous swain, on the other hand, does not forget an appointment with his sweetheart, or if he does, he is likely to find that she holds him to account for this unconscious sign of neglect of her, just as though it had been a consciously intended one. It is not hard to guess that a young man had some hesitation about embarking on marriage if he tells us that, while driving to his wedding, he stopped for a traffic light, and only when it had changed did he realize that he had stopped for a green light instead of a red one.

Another rather transparent example, which might be called a *symptomatic action* rather than a slip of any sort, was furnished by a patient whose appointment had been canceled for his analyst's convenience. The patient found himself somewhat at loose ends during the time that was usually occupied by coming for his treatment, and decided to try out a pair of antique dueling pistols that he had recently bought. So at the time when he would ordinarily have been lying on the analyst's couch, he was shooting a dueling pistol at a target! Even without the patient's associations, one would feel fairly safe in assuming that he was angry at his analyst for having failed to see him that day.

It should be added that, as in the case of dreams, Freud was able, by applying the psychoanalytic technique, to show that unconscious mental activity plays a role in the production of all slips, not just ones in which the significance of such activity is readily apparent, as is true of the examples offered above.

Another easily demonstrable bit of evidence for the proposition that unconscious processes are of significance in mental life is the following. The motives for one's behavior may often be obvious to an observer, though unknown to oneself. Examples of this are familiar from clinical and personal experience. It may be very obvious from her behavior, for instance, that a mother is dominating and demanding toward her child at the same time that she believes herself to be the most self-sacrificing of mothers, who wants only to do what is best for her child with no thought of her own wishes. I think most of us would be ready to assume that this woman had an unconscious desire to dominate and control her child, despite not only her unawareness, but even her vigorous denial of any such desire. Another, somewhat amusing example is the pacifist who is ready to quarrel violently with anyone who contradicts the view that violence is always to be avoided on principle. It seems obvious that, in such case, conscious pacifism is accompanied by an unconscious desire to fight—the very thing that is consciously condemned.

So far we have used examples from normal mental life as evidence for the existence of unconscious mental processes. In fact, however, the importance of unconscious mental activity was first and foremost demonstrated by Freud in the case of symptoms of mentally ill patients. As a result of his discoveries, the idea that such symptoms have a meaning unknown to the patient is by now so generally accepted and understood that it hardly requires illustration. If a patient has a hysterical blindness, we naturally assume that there is something that she/he unconsciously does not wish to see, or that his/her conscience forbids him/her to look at. It is true that it is by no means always easy to ascertain the unconscious meaning of a symptom, and that the unconscious determinants of even a single symptom may be very many and quite complex, so that even if one can guess correctly about its meaning, the guess is only a part, and sometimes a small part, of the whole truth. This is immaterial for our present purpose, however, which is simply to indicate by illustration various sources of evidence for our two fundamental propositions. We believe today, first, that events in mental life are always causally related by their meaning and, second, that consciousness, though an important characteristic of the operations of the mind, is by no means a necessary one. We believe that it need not and often does not attach even to mental operations that are decisive in determining a person's behavior, or to those that are most complex and most precise in their nature. Such operations—even complex and decisive ones—may be quite unconscious.

APPENDIX 3

The unpleasurable affects that trigger mental conflict are of two kinds, anxiety and depressive affect. A sensation of unpleasure plus ideas that one, or more than one, calamity will happen is the hallmark of anxiety. A sensation of unpleasure plus ideas that one, or more than one, calamity has happened is the defining characteristic of depressive affect.

Prior to the publication of my articles on the subject (Brenner 1974a, 1974b, 1974c, 1975), anxiety was considered to be the only affect that triggers mental conflict (Freud 1926). What kind of data support my reformulation?

The following case material is of a sort that is familiar to every analyst from clinical experience. Thus, it not only illustrates the role of depressive affect in psychic conflict; it also indicates how abundant are the psychoanalytic data that demonstrate its role.

A patient in his mid-twenties, as he lay on the couch, would often pick at a sore on his hands or face, finger an old scar, rub a shoulder that had been injured some years earlier, or give some other indication of pain or injury. His attention was repeatedly directed to this behavior, and it gradually became apparent that all these gestures were unconsciously intended to gain my sympathy. In each case he had either told me or was about to tell me of actions or wishes that made him feel guilty and of which he believed that I, too, disapproved. His sores and injuries were unconscious evidence that he had already punished himself enough for his misdeeds and that he should be pitied and coddled rather than blamed and hated, as he expected to be.

As the originally unconscious motivation of his behavior on the couch emerged, it became apparent that it was a transference to the analysis of a pattern of behavior established well before his adolescence. Whenever he was engaged in aggressive or competitive behavior, he tended to injure himself, to make himself fail or lose, or both. Eventually it was possible in the course of his analysis for him to be conscious of daydreams that had previously been unconscious or had been briefly conscious but soon repressed. These daydreams accompanied every ambitious, competitive action he undertook. In them he imagined himself confronted by an older man who was invariably more powerful than he, whether physically or by virtue of his station in life. The main business of the daydream was a violent conflict between the patient and his opponent that always ended with the patient's being defeated. Sometimes the defeat was physical, sometimes not, but it was invariably complete. There was never any question who had won.

At the same time, it became possible to understand the unconscious meaning of a repetitive element of his nocturnal dreams. He remembered only a small fraction of his dreams, but of the ones he did remember, many had to do with fighting with other men. These dreams probably began in latency or, at the latest, in early adolescence. In them the patient was always inhibited in attacking his opponents and was often unable to defend himself effectively. He could never strike an opponent forcefully, either with his fists or with a weapon. If he had a gun, it would not fire, and often he could not even run away.

There was evidence from many sources, therefore—from his behavior during analytic sessions, from his past and present difficulties in every competitive situation, from his daydreams and from his nocturnal dreams—that this patient both inhibited and punished himself for his competitive wishes, wishes directed unconsciously toward his powerful father and also, as it turned out, toward an older brother, who was the principal conscious enemy of his childhood.

What part was played by anxiety in all of this and what part by depressive affect? In those real-life situations in which the patient inhibited his competitive wishes, as well as in the dreams in which he could not fight effectively, anxiety clearly played the role psychoanalytic theory customarily assigns to it. In each such instance, a competitive wish was equated unconsciously with a murderous childhood wish to surpass and supplant his father or older brother. This aroused fear of retaliation, of loss of love, and of object loss—in his case, of being sent away forever—and he defended himself against his frightening wishes by a kind of reaction formation. He demonstrated that he was weak, stupid, ineffectual, and not to be taken seriously as a competitor. One can guess that he unconsciously castrated himself; indeed, fantasies of actual castration did occasionally become conscious at times of intense conflict over his competitive, murderous wishes.

But anxiety and defenses against frightening, competitive wishes do not suffice to explain all the patient's behavior. When he ached, when he, at first unconsciously, begged to be coddled, when, after analysis had progressed further, he wept bitter tears of misery, he no longer *feared* he would be unloved; he was sure that he *was* unloved. His yearning to be coddled, which meant, unconsciously, to be forgiven, did not stem from anxiety, but from a variety of depressive affect that best fits under the heading of remorse.

This aspect of his conflicts emerged even more clearly when, for example, he failed an important examination, when he was refused advancement in his career, or when I left him briefly, either to go on vacation or for some other reason. On those occasions, his behavior and associations during his analytic sessions revealed that he was making great efforts to remain unaware of his misery or to counteract it in some other way. What was intolerable was to be conscious of how miserable he was, to know how he really felt. When his career suffered a check, for instance, he persuaded himself that he had been wrong to choose the career in the first place, that his true interests lay elsewhere, that the thing for him to do was to recognize his basic mistake and to rectify it by pursuing a different career or a different style of life altogether. Perhaps it was silly to pursue any career. Perhaps the only sensible way of life was the one some of his friends pursued: to despise the conventional ambitions of bourgeois morality and to wander about the world enjoying life as it came.

The defensive function of the attitude expressed by this train of thought is obvious. On the occasions when it occurred, it may be noted, it never succeeded in dispelling the patient's misery. It merely mitigated it. When its defensive function was interpreted to him, the patient's response was, "What should I do? Burst into tears?"

His usual response to my leaving him was more successful in avoiding any awareness of his misery. With great enthusiasm, he would make vacation plans himself, plans that expressed the idea that, far from feeling lonely and unhappy at my absence, he was eager to get away and glad of the an opportunity to do so, either to visit a friend or to take a trip with one. In other words, his reaction to my leaving was his way of assuring himself that he was happy, not unhappy, that he did not wish to accompany me, that he had his own place to go to, his own trip to take. As might be expected, it was also an unconscious way of taking revenge on me by being the active rather than the passive one of the two of us.

What is one to conclude from all this? First of all, as has already been noted, some of the patient's reactions to his unconsciously murderous and competitive wishes are readily understandable as defenses triggered by anxiety. In other instances, however, the psychological determinants and motives of his defenses are not understandable on that basis. In those cases, the patient was not unconsciously afraid of what would happen as a result of his wish to supplant his father and brother. He was convinced that he had indeed been punished for wishing to supplant them and for other bad wishes. His defenses were motivated not by a need to avoid or minimize anxiety, but by a need to deny or put an end to his misery and unhappiness. Thus, while anxiety played the role customarily assigned to it in some of this patient's conflicts, in other conflicts, or in other aspects of the same conflicts, it was a variety of depressive affect—misery, unhappiness, or remorse—that gave rise to defense and compromise formation.

To repeat, whenever satisfaction of a childhood pleasure-seeking wish arouses unpleasure, the unpleasure is either anxiety, depressive affect, or a mixture or combination of the two. By anxiety is meant unpleasure plus ideas of danger, i.e., of an impending calamity. By depressive affect is meant unpleasure plus ideas of a calamity not of the future, but of the past. In some cases, the two affects are, for practical purposes, indistinguishable. When they can be distinguished, as they usually can be, it is important that the distinction be made.

As noted earlier, the ideational content of the calamities referred to fall under four headings: object loss, loss of love, genital injury (= castration), and retribution or punishment. When a patient complains of fear of death, of dissolution, of merging with another, of loss of identity, of emptiness, etc., the complaint should not be taken at face value, as though it were a true, endopsychic perception. Such complaints or reports are *symptoms*. Each is a compromise formation among the pleasure-seeking wishes, the unpleasure, and the defensive efforts that constitute the patient's conflict(s). It is not a *description* of part or all of the patient's psychopathology. Application of the psychoanalytic method, when it is possible to apply it, will reveal the complaint(s) to be consequences of the patient's psychopathology, rather than descriptions of it; consequences that can be properly understood and evaluated only after they have been analyzed.

Until evidence to the contrary appears, the calamities that figure importantly in conflicts that result from the pleasure-seeking wishes of childhood should be limited to object loss, loss of love, castration, and retribution and/or punishment. These calamities assume positions of importance in mental life in sequence rather than all together. Object loss begins to play a role before loss of love, while ideas of genital injury and/or inadequacy (= castration) begin to play their part later than either of the other two. For this reason, each calamity is sometimes considered to be phase specific. Object loss is considered to be specific to the oral phase, loss of love to the anal phase, and castration to the genital phase. This schema has its value if it is understood to apply to the approximate stage of development at which the calamity first assumes importance. It must be kept clearly in mind, however, that once it has become important, each calamity remains so throughout the remainder of childhood and of adult life. Nor is each calamity kept separate from the other two. On the contrary, all three become and remain intimately interrelated.

It is a mistake to suppose that the importance of object loss or loss of love as sources of unpleasure in connection with pleasure-seeking wishes is limited to the first two and a half years of life, that is, to the so-called preoedipal period. Nothing is further from the truth. Both play a major role throughout each subsequent period of life as well. For example, every analyst knows what a calamity it is for a child in a later period of development to lose a parent or a parent's love, for whatever reason. Nor is it any novelty to discover, for instance, that a boy of four or five fears losing his father's love because this means to him that the danger of castration is made greater and more immediate.

Just as fear of loss of love and castration can be inseparable calamities in a child's mind, so, too, can depressive affect, whose ideational content is loss of love, be inseparable from depressive affect with the ideational content of phallic inferiority. For example, a boy's depressive affect over the small size of his penis relative to his father's can be intensified by the conviction that, because of it, there is no hope that his mother will ever love him best. Equally common is the conviction of girls that their lack of a penis is proof that their mothers do not or did not love them. In short, analytic experience supports the conclusion that, in the great majority of individuals, if not in every case, the calamities of childhood become intimately interwoven, so intimately that even to discuss each separately does some injustice to the true state of affairs by offering a somewhat artificial scheme of the place of each in psychic life.

In particular, the available relevant evidence supports the conclusion that the appearance of depressive affect is not related exclusively to object loss. It can have as its ideational content any or all of the calamities of childhood, just as anxiety can. To repeat what has already been said, the difference between the two affects is not defined by the nature of the calamity involved. The difference lies in a temporal factor. If a calamity is anticipated, if it lies in the future, the affect is anxiety. If the calamity has already happened, if it lies in the past, the affect is depressive affect. This must be kept in mind if one hopes to achieve a correct understanding of the psychodynamics of depressive illness.

APPENDIX 4

Every student of psychoanalysis is familiar with the traditional list of so-called defense mechanisms: repression, reaction formation, turning from active to passive, turning against oneself, condensation, displacement, projection, identification, identification with an aggressor, denial, and negation. Some years ago, I suggested that the time had come for a major, even a radical revision of this part of psychoanalytic theory, a revision based on a reappraisal of the psychoanalytic data having to do with psychic conflict (Brenner 1975b). These data indicate that whatever ensues in mental life that results in a diminution of anxiety or depressive affect associated with the sexual and aggressive wishes of childhood belongs under the heading of *defense*.

Defenses are not special mechanisms of the mind (A. Freud 1936). Defense is an aspect of mental functioning that is definable only in terms of its consequence: the reduction of anxiety and/or depressive affect associated with the sexual and aggressive wishes of childhood. In fact, the same aspects of mental functioning that one observes clinically in the psychoanalytic situation as defenses against the sexual and aggressive wishes that originate in early childhood serve the purpose at other times of furthering the gratification of those wishes.

To discuss defense in terms of *defense mechanisms* is wrong. To do so implies that there are special mechanisms of defense, mechanisms that are used for defense and for nothing else. This is not the case. To do so also implies that only some mental mechanisms are used for defense, and that there are other mental mechanisms that are not ever used for defense, which is also incorrect. Mental mechanisms (= the entire range of thought processes) are all-purpose. There are none that are used for defense alone. All can be and are used at times to mediate gratification of pleasure-seeking wishes, and at other times to oppose them and to prevent their satisfaction (Brenner 1976). Whatever is useful for the purpose can be used defensively, as, for example, any perception, an alteration of attention or of awareness, fantasy formation, a refusal to be serious, a lack of conviction, or an attitude of make-believe. Anything that comes under the heading of normal mental functioning or development can be used defensively. Modes of defense are as diverse as psychic life itself.

Despite their diverse nature, however, there is something that all modes of defense have in common. This is opposition to the sexual and aggressive wishes of childhood that arouse anxiety or opposition to the affects of anxiety and depressive affect themselves. To say this is to do no more than to restate the definition of *defense*. But reiteration in this form calls attention to something that is often overlooked, which is that there is in defense, by definition, an element of denial or negation in the colloquial meaning of those words. Every defense against a sexual or aggressive wish that arouses anxiety and/or depressive affect is a way of saying "No" to some aspect of it.

Take repression, for example. What does it mean to say that a typical childhood fantasy, for instance, a young boy's wish to replace father in mother's bed and be her husband, is defended against by repression, in whole or in part? The wish, part of which can be expressed by the words "I want to marry Mommy," does not disappear. It is, however, excluded from awareness. As far as the boy himself is concerned, he does not want to marry Mommy. What is more, he no longer remembers he ever did want to marry her. If asked in later life, "Do you want to marry your mother?" he would answer, quite sincerely, "No, I do not." If asked, "Did you ever want to marry her?" he would answer, "Never," just as sincerely, despite the fact that, as we know, the wish to marry her has persisted and is still present in a dynamically active form. In other words, repression is a way of saying "No" to a wish and its associated memories.

So, also, is displacement, when used defensively. If the same boy, in addition to repressing his incestuous wishes for his mother, displaces them, or part of them, onto an aunt or a schoolteacher, his conscious conviction is "I want to marry Aunt Jane (or Mrs. Smith), not Mommy."

The same is true of reaction formation. Should a young boy quarrel with his mother in order—at least in part—to defend against his incestuous wishes for her, the defensive function of his quarreling can be expressed by the words "I do not love her; I *hate* her."

Similarly, if identification is used defensively by a boy who imagines himself to be his baby sibling in order to defend against incestuous wishes for his mother, the defensive aspect of his identification has the meaning, "I do not want to marry Mommy and make babies with her, like Daddy. I want to be her baby and have her hold me and pet me." In this illustration, the pleasure-seeking wish to be held and petted also serves a defensive function against phallic, incestuous wishes, as they would if the defensive identification were with mother herself rather than with baby.

Repression, displacement, reaction formation, and identification are all familiar methods of defense. To take a less familiar method of defense, Arlow (1959) called attention to the fact that, in the experience of déjà vu, a factually incorrect belief serves a defensive function. That is to say, he called attention to the fact that an individual who is convinced that he has already been through something which is, in fact, happening to him for the first time is avoiding anxiety by saying to himself, in effect, "Don't worry. The calamity you are always afraid will happen will not happen this time either."

In such cases, a disturbance of reality testing serves a defensive function. In some dreams, however, the reverse is the case. It is an improvement in reality testing that is used for defensive purposes. When a dreamer has the reassuring thought, "This is just a dream," it serves the function of avoiding the anxiety and/or depressive affect associated with the calamitous fantasies that seemed real a few moments before (Arlow and Brenner 1964).

The examples I have just given are schematized and much simplified. They are nevertheless faithful to the facts of psychic life. Whatever example of defense one may choose will illustrate and support the correctness of the generalization that to defend against a childhood sexual or aggressive wish is to deny or negate it in some way. Denial, in the colloquial sense, is intrinsic to all defense.

It is important to specify that this is true in the colloquial sense for the reason that the word *denial* also has a sense that is technical, a sense that is strictly psychoanalytic. In this sense, the word refers to the defensive distortion of one's perception of some aspect of one's environment, of what is usually called external reality. It is misleading to extend the term to include defensive distortion or disavowal of one's own wishes, affects, memories, etc., since, as we have just seen, every defense denies something. Unless the term *denial* is limited to the usage A. Freud (1936) proposed, it has no special or technical meaning whatsoever. It is merely a synonym for defense (Brenner 1973).

The assertion that no mental function or mechanism is exclusively or specially defensive may be illustrated as follows. A child who "forgets" having been told not to masturbate has repressed the parental prohibition in the service of gratifying a pleasure-seeking wish, not as a means of defense. There is no doubt that repression very often serves the purpose of defense. What I add here is that it often can and does also serve the purpose of facilitating the gratification of a pleasure-seeking wish.

The same is true of every other familiar mode of defense, as well as of those that are less familiar. Examples lie close to hand for the very reasons mentioned earlier. When unpleasure is aroused or threatens to be aroused, one does whatever one can to avoid or to reduce it. When one desires gratification and pleasure, one does whatever one can to achieve it. What one can conceivably do is the same in either case. *It is the function served by what one does that determines whether it is properly called defense.* Properly speaking, a defense can be identified only by the purpose or function it serves in the psychic economy, i.e., the function of opposing or warding off some psychic impulse or tendency that has aroused anxiety or depressive affect. It is a mistake to define or identify *defense* primarily by the method used to achieve the purpose of defense. Repression, reaction formation, regression, displacement, etc., are defenses only when they are used to ward off something that arouses anxiety and/or depressive affect.

An example may help to clarify the points at issue. It is not rare for a love affair to start in the following way. One person sees another who is sexually attractive, under circumstances that preclude an immediate, direct approach. Instead, before actually approaching the future partner, he or she has a pleasurable daydream in which the two are already sexually united. Such a fantasy involves projection—in this case, attributing one's own sexual desire and excitement to another. The attribution enhances and facilitates gratification of drive derivatives through the fantasy of which it is a part. Here is an instance, then, where projection functions to further gratification, rather than functioning defensively. At the same time, it must be recognized that the fantasy itself, pleasurable though it is, is a compromise formation. It is compounded of childhood sexual and aggressive wishes and of defenses to eliminate the unpleasure associated with them. A fantasy, like a symptom, is a compromise formation. In some fantasies projection serves the function of defense, while in others, it furthers gratification.

A realization of the full import of these facts involves a reevaluation of two familiar concepts in psychoanalytic theory. One is the concept that each patient has a characteristic and limited repertory of defenses. The other is the concept that defenses disappear as a consequence of psychoanalytic work.

As for the first of these, it is an idea that applies only to particular symptoms, not to an individual's total mental functioning. To repeat, everyone's defensive repertory is as broad as his or her range of mental functioning. Particular symptoms, however, do involve characteristic defensive patterns, sometimes by definition.

It is only if attention is concentrated on one or more prominent symptoms or on a prominent aspect of the patient's transference reaction, while the remainder of the patient's mental functioning is ignored, that one can make out a case that he or she has a limited repertory of defenses.

For example, displacement is involved in every phobia. So is avoidance, by definition. The defensive "repertory" of every phobic patient's *symptoms,* therefore, includes avoidance and displacement. If, as often happens, attention in the analytic situation is focused on the patient's phobic symptom(s), his or her defenses may seem to be limited to those and other, related defenses, since they are the ones that appear repeatedly and must be dealt with over and over again. Likewise, if a patient has many prominent somatic symptoms of psychic origin, then, by definition, conversion of psychic conflicts into somatic manifestations plays a role in the dynamics of those symptoms. Again, there are patients with delusional symptomatology. It is not difficult to identify projection operating defensively in many such patients, since delusions so often involve attributing one's wishes, fears, etc., to others in order to minimize the anxiety and/or depressive affect associated with one's wishes, fears, and misery.

So to speak of a characteristic repertory of defenses is really to say only that prominent neurotic symptoms and/or character traits are apt to be persistent in any patient, are apt to be prominent in that patient's analytic material, and are apt to require repeated analysis and interpretation in the course of that patient's analysis. As a matter of practical necessity, one focuses analytic attention principally on such troublesome features of a patient's life and, by extension, on the defenses involved in their genesis and dynamics. However, if one includes in one's assessment of each patient's defenses not just those that are part of his or her major symptomatology, but also those that are involved in the patient's dreams, fantasies, ambitions, plans—in short, in the entire gamut of the patient's mental life, normal as well as pathological—one sees immediately how inapplicable is the concept of a limited repertory of defenses. It is not that patients show a limited repertory of defensive methods; it is that one or another symptom, one or another character trait, or one or another transference manifestation is characterized by a special method of defense.

As for the idea that defenses disappear in the course of analysis, the following remarks are in order. In the course of a successful analysis, defensive patterns change. Of this there is no doubt. However, particular modes of defense neither disappear, nor do they change in any regular, uniform, or predictable way as a result of analysis. What happens as analysis proceeds is not that defenses change in a progressive way, but that the patient's *compromise formations* change in a progressive way. By this I mean that, as analysis progresses, the patient's compromise formations change in such a way that the sexual and aggressive wishes in question are less disguised, less distorted, and can be gratified with pleasure to an increasing degree. Which is the same as saying that when analysis is successful, pathological compromise formations give way to normal ones (Brenner 1975b, 1976). An example will be useful in clarifying these statements.

The patient was a 29-year-old woman who had been in analysis for six years at the time of the episode to be reported. The relevant data concerning her preanalytic and analytic history are these. Prior to analysis, she had had sexual relations only with women. Her behavior during these affairs was dominated by her unconscious need to deny (1) sexual feelings for her father, (2) jealous and hostile wishes toward her mother and her older, married sister, and (3) her rage and humiliation that she did not have a penis. Thus, for example, while having sex with a woman, she had the fantasy, which was unconscious prior to analysis, that she herself had a penis, that she was a man in a sexual embrace with a woman.

In the course of her analysis, the patient had sexual intercourse with men for the first time. During intercourse, she sometimes had conscious fantasies of controlling her partner's penis. At other times, she imagined that his penis was part of her body rather than of his. These heterosexual affairs were interspersed with homosexual ones, each of which was initiated by her unconscious need to defend against sexual longings for her analyst.

These she warded off by assuming the male role in a homosexual relationship, just as, before analysis, she had warded off her unconscious sexual wishes for her father.

At the time with which we are concerned, the patient was once more involved in a homosexual relationship. It had begun some months before, just as her analyst had left for his vacation. Though consciously struggling to give up her current girlfriend, she was obviously resentful of her analyst and was trying to provoke him. She complained indignantly that he behaved unfairly toward her and that he never gave her her due.

During one session, when she was arguing with herself about giving up her girlfriend, she paused frequently, obviously waiting for her analyst to speak. He finally did intervene to say that she was trying to get him to order her to give up her girlfriend so that she could rebel, just as she had so often tried to get her parents to take a position she could use as an excuse for rebelling against them. He did not add to this interpretation in words something that the patient well understood, because it had been interpreted to her many times in the past on appropriate occasions: that her anger at her parents throughout her life and at her analyst now was fueled by the fact that she did not have a penis, and by the fact that neither her father nor her analyst loved her as she was sure they would have if she had been the boy her father had hoped for before she was born.

Thus this interpretation, as the patient understood it, had to do with her wish for love and for a penis in the transference situation and with the fact that it was the frustration of those wishes that made her feel anger toward her analyst—anger she attributed to him, via projection, lest she feel guilty. This interpretation appeared to have a considerable effect on the patient. During the next week, she showed the following changes:

1. She discontinued the homosexual affair.
2. She was more feminine in dress and manner.
3. She began to date a man.

4. She asked an older, male colleague, an obvious father figure, to accept her as a pupil, even though she said in advance that she was sure he would refuse.
5. She was much less angry at her analyst and was aware that she wished to be close to him.
6. She had a frightening dream, the associations to which led to thoughts of being sexually excited while on her analyst's couch. It should be noted that she did not actually feel sexually excited either in connection with those thoughts or at any other time when she was on the couch.
7. She became aware that she was angry at her mother, at her older sister, who was her lifelong rival, and at a married female friend.
8. She recalled longing to be close to her father when she was five years old.

Here is an instance of analytic progress. The patient improved professionally and changed in her sexual behavior as a result of a correct interpretation, properly timed and preceded by much previous interpretive work along the same line. What were the changes in the patient's defenses in this particular instance?

It will be recalled that, before the interpretation, the patient was not conscious of love and sexual longing for her analyst. Instead, she was angry at him. In other words, her loving and sexual wishes were defended against, in part at least, by anger. The same sort of defense warded off her anger and jealousy toward women whom she saw as rivals. She was not aware of negative feelings toward such women. Instead, she was carrying on a love affair with a woman for whom she yearned and by whom she was sexually aroused.

She dealt with her castrative and vengeful wishes toward men in a different way. She felt mistreated by her analyst. She felt that he shortchanged her. In other words, she projected her anger onto him. Still another defense involved in her unconscious effort to deal with her castrative and vengeful wishes toward men was identification. She played the part of a man in the sexual affair she was having.

Finally, the memory that she longed for closeness with her father when she was five had long since succumbed to repression, a repression that lifted only after the interpretation was made.

This account of the patient's defenses is far from complete, but it will suffice for my present purpose. If the substitution of anger for love and vice versa be called *reaction formation,* for convenience in describing it, we can say that, before the interpretation in question, the patient was using repression, reaction formation, projection, and identification as defenses against certain of her drive derivatives. How were they changed by the interpretation?

First of all, the patient's pattern of reaction formation changed. She gave up her homosexual affair and began dating men. She also expressed anger at female rivals on several occasions—her mother, her older sister, and her married friend—while she was less angry at her analyst than she had been and was aware of wishing to be close to him. In other words, the reaction formations of love for women in order to ward off anger at them, and of anger at men in order to ward off love for them, were both much diminished.

Second, repression of some memories of her sexual longing for her father was undone. At the same time, we may safely assume that many other, related memories remained repressed. That is, repression was diminished rather than wholly undone.

Third, identification with the older, admired colleague who was her new teacher clearly played a role in her becoming his pupil.

Fourth, she defended against her sexual wishes for her analyst, which gave rise to anxiety in her dream, by experiencing them as ideas, as mere inferences from her association to her dream. This sort of defense is usually called isolation of affect.

Finally, her anger at mother and sister was, in part, displaced to her married friend.

It will be recalled that, prior to her improvement, the patient was using repression, reaction formation, projection, and identification as defenses. She progressed analytically as a result of interpretation. What were the changes in her defensive pattern? How can one generalize about them? Can one say that pathogenic defenses disappeared, or that they were replaced by normal ones, or even that more infantile defenses were replaced by less infantile ones?

None of these questions can be answered in the affirmative. The patient's defenses neither disappeared nor became either normal or more mature.

For example, a defensive identification with men was present both before and after the interpretation. Before the interpretation, this identification decisively influenced her sexual behavior. She had wooed a woman and was engaged in a sexual relationship with her, a relationship in which the patient played the part of a man. After the interpretation, the same identification was expressed in her vocational behavior. She took steps to become the pupil of a man she admired in order to learn his skills and to be able to use the tools of his profession—tools, it may be added, that had for her a phallic significance. This is to say that, both before and after the interpretation, certain aspects of her behavior were motivated by identification with a man, an identification that served to defend against her feminine, oedipal wishes, as well as gratifying her masculine ones.

That there was a significant change in her behavior, no one can doubt. She became more mature. One can fairly say that she became more normal, since before the interpretation her masculine identification was expressed in a homosexual affair, while after the interpretation, it was expressed in her relationship with an older man, her teacher, whom she planned to emulate vocationally in a realistically rewarding, socially desirable way. But what of the defense of identification itself? She still identified with a man. The tools of her teacher's profession were transparently phallic symbols, and to learn to use them expressed her unconscious fantasy that she had a penis. Can one say her use of identification as a defense was any less infantile or more normal after the interpretation than before it, even though the compromise formation of which it was a part was certainly more mature and normal?

Similarly, repression was lifted in one respect following the interpretation. Certain sexual memories from age five emerged for the first time in her adult life. Yet repression intensified in another respect, since the patient's castrative wishes toward her analyst were repressed after the interpretation, whereas they had been warded off by projection before it. In this case, then, projection disappeared after the interpretation, but repression, a potentially pathogenic defense by any standard, appeared in its place.

If one looks at what I have called the patient's reaction formations, one is faced with similar data. The patient's use of love to defend against jealous anger was much less after the interpretation than it was before, but it was replaced, in part at least, by displacement. The reverse—the use of hate to ward off love—was partly replaced by isolation of affect, a defense so often found in patients with obsessional symptoms.

It is apparent that, in this example of analytic progress, the patient's defenses neither disappeared nor became, in and of themselves, less pathogenic or more mature. What happened in fact was this. There were certain wishes the patient had to defend against to avoid or minimize anxiety and/or depressive affect. These included the following: affection for her analyst; longing for his love; memories of affection and longing for her father's love when she was a child; the wish to be closely associated with an older, admired man and to be his pupil; the wish to attract men and to have sexual intercourse with them; and anger at women rivals. All of them were related to conflict-laden sexual and aggressive wishes of her childhood. Before the interpretation, they could not be tolerated; they aroused too much unpleasure. After the interpretation, the patient's reaction to them was less defensive in the sense that the resulting compromise between wish and defense allowed more in the way of gratification.

The change was not so complete that no defenses were necessary—quite the contrary. The patient's reactions to her sexual and aggressive wishes after the interpretation were no less a compromise between wish and defense than they had been before. Defenses against the wishes were as easily identifiable after the interpretation as they had been before it. The new compromise formation represented analytic progress, but it was still a compromise formation, for all that.

I hope this rather lengthy illustration has served to persuade the reader of the fact that, in the course of analysis, defenses neither disappear nor become progressively more normal (less pathological) or more mature. As for the idea that repression, reaction formation, or any other mental capacity that is at times used defensively can ever disappear, no illustration or further discussion should be necessary to demonstrate how incorrect and inapposite this is. A particular instance of the defensive use of any mental "mechanism" may cease, but it is out of the question to imagine that the mechanism as such can disappear as a result of analysis.

I have been concerned so far with defense as an aspect of mental functioning that is defined by its consequence, the consequence being the avoidance, disappearance, or mitigation of anxiety and/or depressive affect developing in association with sexual and aggressive wishes that originated in childhood. I turn now to another topic, namely, the targets of defense, that is to say, to the question, "What is warded off or defended against to avoid or minimize these unpleasurable affects?"

Freud's answer was that, when a sexual or aggressive wish arouses anxiety, the essence of defense is opposition to it. If an incestuous wish arouses anxiety, the wish is defended against, or warded off, in one way or another. If the defensive effort is successful, anxiety is avoided or disappears. One cannot dispute the correctness of Freud's formulation. Confirmation of it is available daily from the analysis of every patient. It is, however, but a partial answer, as the following discussion will show.

Defense proceeds in accordance with the pleasure-unpleasure principle. It is the unpleasure of anxiety and of depressive affect that triggers defense, and this unpleasure is tied to a particular ideational content, i.e., to one or more of the familiar calamities of childhood. It is the connection between a wish and a calamity or calamities that gives rise to defense in accordance with the pleasure-unpleasure principle. A childhood wish does not give rise to unpleasure directly. It does so because it is associated in the child's mind with ideas of calamity.

Since the function of defense is to eliminate unpleasure or, at least, to reduce it to a minimum, one would expect that this could be accomplished in more than one way. One way is the one Freud described, namely, to oppose the drive derivative—to say "No" to it. Another possible way would be to oppose or ward off not the wish per se, but the anxiety and/or depressive affect aroused by the wish. Thus one can imagine that anxiety and/or depressive affect could be lessened in any of three ways. A defense might say "No" to the unpleasure of the affect, to its ideational content, or to both at the same time. Psychoanalytic clinical data demonstrate that all these possibilities do, in fact, occur.

I believe that Fenichel's (1939) description of the counterphobic attitude is the first extensive exposition of the fact that defense can reduce or eliminate anxiety by taking as its target the anxiety associated with a wish rather than the wish itself. (See also Brenner 1975b, 1979.)

Again, one must bear in mind that a symptom is a compromise formation. It is never merely a defense. For instance, being counterphobic by becoming a daredevil and delighting in doing what is dangerous is a symptom. It is a compromise formation and, as such, it serves to gratify drive derivatives as well as to eliminate or to minimize anxiety. Being a daredevil may, for example, gratify an unconscious masochistic wish. However, turning anxiety into pleasure, which is the essence of the counterphobic attitude, is a way of eliminating unpleasure that is quite different from defending against a wish that arouses anxiety and/or depressive affect. Instead of the wish being the target of defense, the affect itself is the target—in this case by denying the unpleasure altogether. Often the reversal of affect (pleasure instead of unpleasure) is buttressed by narcissistic, exhibitionistic gratification, as when a daredevil performs publicly for applause and approval. Often it is buttressed by identification, by a conscious or unconscious fantasy of being an admired and envied rival.

Doubtless there are other ways, more subtle and more specifically individual, by which such a reversal of affect can be buttressed or reinforced. Whatever the means used, it is the affect associated with the calamity that is the target of defense, not the wish.

When anxiety or depressive affect is itself the target of defense, as noted earlier, it is often the case that both the sensation of unpleasure and the ideational content, which together constitute that affect, are defended against. In the example just given, for instance, a daredevil's unconscious castration anxiety may be represented by parachute jumping, with its attendant mortal danger. In other words, the counterphobic person may become a sky diver. If he does, part of his defense is to transform anxiety into pleasurable exhilaration. For him, to leap into space has become a source of joy and pleasure. Another part of his defense, however, is to disguise the ideational content of his infantile calamity by substituting body for penis and sky diving for castration. The calamity a sky diver consciously faces is not that of losing his penis, but that of smashing his body to bits, like Icarus, on the earth below. Still another part of his defense is likely to be to study the technique of sky diving, to buy the best equipment, to fold his parachute himself, to jump only in fine weather, etc.

Daredevils rarely seek psychoanalysis. I recall but one such patient in my own practice. The defensive pattern they illustrate is by no means a rarity, however. It is common for patients and, for that matter, for many who are not patients, to do something to "prove" they need not be afraid or, indeed, that they *are* not afraid, when it is obvious that they are very afraid indeed. In other words, it is common for patients and others to diminish anxiety by repressing, denying, projecting, or otherwise warding off either the unpleasure, the ideational content, or both, that are associated with object loss, loss of love, and/or castration.

A life-threatening example would be a patient with a myocardial infarct who refused to stay in bed. Another example, but one within the range of normality, would be a timid schoolboy who took up football or boxing. In fact, what is called courage is closely related to what Fenichel (1939) identified as the counterphobic attitude. Thus psychoanalytic data confirm the conventional wisdom of military personnel that courage in combat is the ability to ignore or overcome fear, an aphorism to which psychoanalytic data lend greater depth and a wider applicability than could otherwise have been suspected.

Like anxiety, depressive affect that has as its ideational content one or more of the calamities of childhood can be the target of defense. It, too, can be reduced or eliminated by defending against either its unpleasure, its ideational content, or both (Brenner 1975a).

To deny that a calamity has occurred, when in fact one believes it has, by pretending that it is really a joy; to insist that one feels pleasure rather than unpleasure on account of it, is one of the basic features of pathological elation (mania or hypomania). In any case of pathological elation, much more is involved than reversal of affect of the sort just described. Elation is a syndrome, not a defense. As such it is a compromise formation. It necessarily involves the partial gratification of wishes as well as defense. Nor is a reversal of affect ever the whole of any patient's defensive effort. I do not believe that any instance of pathological elation can be fully or satisfactorily explained as merely a consequence of a patient's denying that a calamity has occurred and thereby turning unpleasure into pleasure as a method of defense. I maintain only that this defensive maneuver is of fundamental importance in every case of pathological elation. It is by no means the whole explanation, but it is an essential element in the dynamics of elation.

APPENDIX 5

Freud's first published exposition of a theory of the mind—or, to use his preferred term, of the mental apparatus—is contained in the seventh chapter of *The Interpretation of Dreams* (Freud 1900). There he suggested that the mind is composed of three systems, for which he proposed the names *Cs.* (= Conscious), *Pcs.* (= Preconscious), and *Ucs.* (= Unconscious). Although he later changed the names and definitions of the systems into which he proposed to divide the mind, the idea that the mind is best understood as a group of functionally identifiable systems, agencies, or structures (the three words are synonymous in this context) is one that he held throughout his life (Arlow and Brenner 1964).

The fact that these systems and structures are, moreover, an aspect of psychoanalytic theory that has won general and unchallenged acceptance by psychoanalysts is attested to by the currency of the terms that Freud introduced at various times to designate the various systems: the conscious, the preconscious, the unconscious, and the ego, the id, the superego. But despite the fact that the idea (= theory) that the mind is best understood as a group of functionally identifiable and separable structures has achieved general acceptance, I believe it is not a valid theory and should be discarded (Brenner 1998).

The related ideas of conflict and compromise formation were what suggested to Freud in the first place that different parts of the mind can be opposed to one another. He discovered very early in his analytic work with patients that psychogenic symptoms have meaning (Freud 1894, 1895). His early observations persuaded him that such patients want to gratify some sexual wish(es) of childhood origin that are inaccessible to consciousness in adult life, and, at the same time, they want to deny, disavow, or suppress those wishes. To explain these findings, he proposed the theory that one part of the mind, the system Ucs., that is inaccessible to consciousness, is bent on gratifying such wishes, and another part, the systems Pcs. and Cs., that are conscious or accessible to consciousness, is opposed to their gratification. Mental conflict and symptom formation are then explainable as the result of conflict between different systems or structures within the mind.

To summarize very briefly, one system or structure, called first the Ucs. and later the *id*, was understood to be concerned with the achievement of pleasurable gratification of sexual and aggressive wishes of childhood origin without delay, and to function without regard to the demands and limitations imposed by the environment (= external reality). Another structure, or group of related functions, called first the Cs.-Pcs. and later the *ego*, was understood to take account of and conform to those very demands and limitations. It was credited with serving the function of controlling—and, when necessary, opposing—the sexual and aggressive wishes of the id. A third structure, the *superego*, was understood to serve the function of erecting and enforcing each individual's moral code of beliefs and behavior. Thus, the clinically observable data of mental conflict are to be explained, according to Freud, by the assumption that the mind is composed of functionally definable and separable structures (= systems, agencies) that may, by their very nature, be opposed to one another.

The fundamental importance attributed to this theoretical concept is underlined by the fact that analysts customarily use it to designate the whole of psychoanalytic theory. Its first version, which divided the mind into Cs., Pcs., and Ucs., gave rise to the term *topographic theory*, generally used by analysts to designate the whole of psychoanalytic theory as it existed prior to 1923, when Freud published *The Ego and the Id*. The second version, which divided the mind into ego, superego, and id, gave rise to the term *structural theory*, which, in its turn, has generally been used to designate the whole of psychoanalytic theory as it has developed subsequent to the publication of *The Ego and the Id*.

The truth is, however, that the theoretical concept that divides the mind into structures, systems, or agencies is but one part of psychoanalytic theory, a part that has been, to be sure, an important and enduring one until now. It is only that part that I consider invalid in light of current knowledge. I am not suggesting that one call into question such aspects of psychoanalytic theory as psychic causality, for example, or the role of unconscious mental processes, or that dreams and symptoms have meaning, or that psychosexual life begins in early childhood, to name but a few of its tenets. I assert only that mental functioning in general—and mental conflict and compromise formation in particular—are not best explained by the theory that the mind is composed of three functionally definable and separable structures (= systems or agencies) called ego, superego, and id.

It should be added that Freud attributed additional distinguishing characteristics to the systems or structures into which he proposed to divide the mind. These will be merely mentioned here, since I assume they are familiar to most readers. (For a fuller discussion, see Arlow and Brenner 1964.) Freud believed that what he called the *id* functions according to what he proposed to call the *primary process*. The id, he posited, is concerned solely with achieving prompt and full gratification of pleasure-seeking wishes of childhood origin. In its functioning (= primary process), it takes no account of external reality, disregards rules of logic, tolerates mutually contradictory ideas, is unconcerned with temporal restraints or demands, and so on. Its way of functioning can be aptly described as being in accord with the demand, "I want what I want and I want it right now!" The id, Freud believed, is a part of the mind that serves the drives and ignores the environment.

The ego, by contrast, was conceived to be as tied to external reality as the id is tied to the individual's pleasure-seeking wishes. The ego, Freud proposed, functions according to the *secondary process*. It obeys the rules of logic, is cognizant of the demands and constraints of the environment and attempts to conform to them, does not tolerate mutually contradictory ideas, is concerned with temporal constraints, and so on. In addition, Freud postulated that what goes on in the id, following the primary process, is nonverbal, while what goes on in the ego, following the secondary process, is verbal.

As is evident from even such a very brief summary as this, the theory of mental agencies embodies Freud's conclusion that what he had discovered about the role of conflict in mental life is best understood if one assumes that one part of the mind functions in an infantile way, while another part functions in a more mature way. Thus, as noted in appendix 1, the systems Pcs. and Cs. were supposed to form only at the beginning of what Freud called the latency period of mental development, and only then to begin to take over control of access to consciousness, the function that they normally performed thereafter.

How consonant is this theory or assumption with observable facts? Let's start with the id. What can be observed in each individual case that can be studied with the help of the psychoanalytic method are that individual's attempts to achieve the pleasurable satisfaction of sexual and aggressive wishes (Brenner 1976, 1982). From the very earliest time of life at which such wishes can be observed, they are anchored in reality. They never, so far as can be observed with the help of the psychoanalytic method, ignore external reality as perceived and understood by the individual at the time of life in question. A child aged three years or thereabouts wants satisfaction from its parent, i.e., from a particular person, and it wants a particular form of physical contact with that person. It does not want "oral gratification," for example. It wants to suck or swallow a particular person's penis or breast. Its wishes are realistic ones, given its state of mental development. They are determined by its experiences and by its thoughts about those experiences. It wants to do or to have done to it what it has observed and/or fantasized being done to or by one or more of the persons of its environment. However illogical and unrealistic its wishes may be by adult standards, they are quite in accord with what the child understands of the real world in which it lives. Associated competitive, murderous, and/or castrative wishes are similarly determinatively influenced by the persons and events of the external world.

Furthermore, such sexual and aggressive wishes cannot be said to be nonverbal. All of them can be formulated in words and are so formulated by each individual, however primitive and immature its verbal capacities may be. All young children certainly have wishes that are irrational and/or unrealistic by adult standards, and that appear so when they persist, as they so often do, into adult life, whether consciously or unconsciously. They were not, however, either irrational or unrealistic at their time of origin. To say that there is a part of the mind, the id, that strives for pleasurable gratification of sexual and aggressive wishes, with no concern for external reality, is wholly at odds with the observable data.

The same is true for the theory that a part of the mind, the ego, exists that is reality bound, that strives to be mature and logical, that is more concerned with its relation to the external world than with achieving pleasurable sexual gratification. Every aspect of mental functioning attributable to what Freud proposed to call the ego is, in fact, a compromise formation that serves the purpose of gratifying pleasure-seeking wishes of childhood origin, as well as the purpose of defending against them (Brenner 1968, 1982, 1997). There is no part of the mind that functions in a mature, logical, realistic way simply because that is the way that part of the mind is designed to function, which is what Freud, and most analysts who followed him, maintain is the case. To be mature in one's thinking, to be logical, to be consistent, to take account of the demands and constraints of the environment, are all behaviors that express conflict and compromise formation originating in the pleasure-seeking wishes of childhood. The most intelligent, highly educated persons may believe religious myths that are obviously unsupported by observable data. Millions of individuals in time of war are united in attributing to the enemy the least acceptable of their own wishes. There is no part of the mind that functions as the ego is supposed to do.

Being logical, mature, and realistic in one's thinking does in itself gratify sexual and aggressive wishes of childhood origin. It may gratify childhood wishes to be as omniscient as one's parents seem to every child to be, to win their praise, or to compete with them or with brothers and sisters. Like all compromise formations, such attitudes and behaviors have a defensive function as well; they may reassure that one is not castrated or otherwise defective, or that one is reasonable and obedient rather than rebelliously antagonistic.

Whatever its origins may be, a mature, logical, and realistic attitude is in every case a compromise formation, as can be demonstrated whenever analysis is possible. Analytic and other data speak against the conclusion that secondary process mentation occurs due to the fact that a part of the mind, the ego, operates by its very nature in a mature, logical, and realistic way. For the mind to operate in the way that Freud called the primary process is often perfectly ego-syntonic (Brenner 1968).

The mind is not best understood in terms of structures or agencies. It is better understood in terms of conflict and compromise formation that occur in accordance with the pleasure-unpleasure principle. There is no mental structure or agency that ignores external reality, nor is there any that by its nature is bound to external reality. (See Brenner 1982.) Any theory to the contrary is invalid. It is not the best conclusion one can draw from the available, relevant data. The theory that is valid in the light of the relevant data that are available at present is what Abend (1994) proposed be called *modern conflict theory*.

REFERENCES

ABEND, S. M. (1994). Personal communication.
ARLOW, J. A. (1959). The structure of the déjà vu experience. *J. Amer. Psychoanal. Assn.*, 7:611-631.
ARLOW, J. A. & BRENNER, C. (1964). *Psychoanalytic Concepts and the Structural Theory.* New York: Int. Univ. Press.
BACON, F. (1620). *Novum Organum,* trans. & ed. P. Urbach & J. Gibson. Chicago, IL: Open Court Publishers, 1993.
BRENNER, C. (1953). An addendum to Freud's theory of anxiety. *Int. J. Psychoanal.*, 34:18-24.
——— (1957a). The nature and development of the concept of repression in Freud's writings. *Psychoanal. Study Child,* 12:19-46.
——— (1957b). The reformulation of the theory of anxiety. In *A General Selection from the Works of Sigmund Freud,* ed. J. Rickman. Garden City, NY: Doubleday.
——— (1968). Archaic features of ego functioning. *Int. J. Psychoanal.*, 49:426-430.
——— (1973). *An Elementary Textbook of Psychoanalysis.* New York: Doubleday/Anchor Books.
——— (1974a). Depression, anxiety, and affect theory. *Int. J. Psychoanal.*, 55:25-32.
——— (1974b). On the nature and development of affects: a unified theory. *Psychoanal. Q.,* 43:532-556.
——— (1974c). Some observations on depression, on nosology, on affects, and on mourning. *J. Geriat. Psychol.,* 7:6-20.
——— (1975a). Affects and psychic conflict. *Psychoanal. Q.,* 44:5-28.
——— (1975b). Alterations in defenses during psychoanalysis. In *The Ernst Kris Study Group of the New York Psychoanalytic Institute, Monograph 6,* ed. B. D. Fine & H. F. Waldhorn. New York: Int. Univ. Press.
——— (1976). *Psychoanalytic Technique and Psychic Conflict.* Madison, CT: Int. Univ. Press.
——— (1979). Depressive affect, anxiety, and psychic conflict in the phallic-oedipal phase. *Psychoanal. Q.,* 48:177-197.
——— (1982). *The Mind in Conflict.* Madison, CT: Int. Univ. Press.
——— (1994). The mind as conflict and compromise formation. *J. Clin. Psychoanal.,* 3:473-488.

——— (1995). Some remarks on psychoanalytic technique. *J. Clin. Psychoanal.*, 4:413-428.
——— (1997). Environmental factors in the development of reality testing. In *The Perverse Transference and Other Matters*, ed. J. L. Ahumada, J. Olagaray, A. K. Richards & A. D. Richards. Northvale, NJ: Aronson.
——— (1998). Beyond the ego and the id revisited. *J. Clin. Psychoanal.*, 7:165-180.
——— (2002). Reflections on psychoanalysis. *J. Clin. Psychoanal.*, 11:7-37.
——— (2004). Creativity and psychodynamics. *Psychoanal. Q.*, 73:511-515.
FARRELL, B. A. (1955). Psychological theory and the belief in God. *Int. J. Psychoanal.*, 36:187-204.
FENICHEL, O. (1939). The counter-phobic attitude. In *The Collected Papers of Otto Fenichel*. New York: Norton, 1954.
FREUD, A. (1936). The ego and the mechanisms of defence. In *The Writings of Anna Freud*, Vol. 2. Madison, CT: Int. Univ. Press.
FREUD, S. (1894). The neuro-psychoses of defence. *S. E.*, 3:43-62.
——— (1895). Further remarks on the neuro-psychoses of defence. *S. E.*, 3:162-188.
——— (1900). *The Interpretation of Dreams*. *S. E.*, 4/5.
——— (1901). *The Psychopathology of Everyday Life*. *S. E.*, 6.
——— (1905). *Three Essays on the Theory of Sexuality*. *S. E.*, 7.
——— (1907). *Delusions and Dreams in Jensen's "Gradiva."* *S. E.*, 9.
——— (1909). Analysis of a phobia in a five-year-old boy. *S. E.*, 10.
——— (1910). *Leonardo da Vinci and a Memory of His Childhood*. *S. E.*, 11.
——— (1917). *Introductory Lectures on Psycho-Analysis*. *S. E.*, 15/16.
——— (1918). From the history of an infantile neurosis. *S. E.*, 17.
——— (1920). *Beyond the Pleasure Principle*. *S. E.*, 18.
——— (1923). *The Ego and the Id*. *S. E.*, 19.
——— (1924). An autobiographical study. *S. E.*, 20.
——— (1926). *Inhibitions, Symptoms and Anxiety*. *S. E.*, 20.
——— (1933). *New Introductory Lectures on Psycho-Analysis*. *S. E.*, 22.
KRIS, E. (1952). *Psychoanalytic Explorations in Art*. Madison, CT: Int. Univ. Press.
SACHS, H. (1942). The community of daydreams. In *The Creative Unconscious*. Cambridge, MA: Sci-Art Publishers.
STRACHEY, J. (1934). The nature of the therapeutic action of psychoanalysis. *Int. J. Psychoanal.*, 15:127-159.

DATE DUE